VOTE
FOR AMERICA

A Common Guide to Electorates

Michael P. Amram

Wisdom Editions
Minneapolis

Wisdom
Editions

Minneapolis

First Edition September 2020
Vote for America: A Common Guide to Electorates.
Copyright © 2020 by Michael P. Amram. All rights reserved.

Printed in the United States of America.
10 9 8 7 6 5 4 3 2 1

ISBN: 978-1-950743-30-8
Cover and book design by Gary Lindberg

VOTE
FOR AMERICA

A Common Guide to Electorates

To John Lewis,
you crossed a bridge to give the other side a voice

CONTENTS

Prologue

Traits are physical and cultural. They are learned by repetition, by mimicry, by perspicacious observation. I learned the concept—the act of voting—quite literally at my mother's knee. In the voting booth, I watched her pull black levers or flip switches corresponding with our candidate's names. In the 1970s, voting was so much simpler; no ovals to fill in completely, staying within the curves. (Today voting is reminiscent of marking the SATs!) I tagged along with my dad to caucuses in school lunchrooms. He organized, chaired, taught and spoke publicly. He was a driving force in Minnesota's third Congressional district for Richfield. He ascended on to the Senate district level, all the way to the riotous 1968 Democratic National Convention. I never inherited his acumen or motivation to seek the top fringes of politics, but I did learn what it is to exercise one's civic responsibility. I never sat idly by and expected anything to change if everyone took for granted their constitutional right to vote. Without a vote on a massive scale, there is virtually no chance America will operate the way those well-intentioned pilgrims once hinted that we might.

Having been adopted, I can't claim that voting is in my DNA. I have no idea how vigilant my biological mother was about voting. My guess is though from having known her for twenty years, she was at least half as political as my mother. I do know that my biological father was active in politics. I am told he worked on the McGovern campaign in 1972. The political impetus was in there, in my DNA and, not unlike democracy itself, the hyper-political parents who adopted me nurtured the seed.

In 1984, I was nineteen years old and facing my first general election as a legal voter. Four years earlier, in 1980, I had cast my fantasy vote for the Carter/Mondale ticket and lost in bitter disappointment, witnessing another shellacking of a Democrat. (In the 1972 campaign, I had watched my mom as a delegate.) Still, implacable as Democrats need to be, I registered for my first legal presidential vote. I was on the voter rolls in Winona, Minnesota, where I had begun college that fall.

1984 Presidential Election

Candidate / running mate	Party	Electoral vote	VAP (voting age pop.)	Popular vote / %
Ronald Reagan/ George H. W. Bush	Republican	525	53.30%	54,455,472/ 58.8
Walter Mondale/ Geraldine Ferraro	Democratic	13		37,577,352/ 40.6

Voting for a woman to foot the ticket was an added attraction to me that year. Now, thirty-six years later, I can again vote for a woman, and a woman of color, on a ticket. In 1984 I felt the ambient tugs of discouragement that lead to apathy, and apathy should never be an option for a taxpaying citizen who values getting the most for his or her hard-earned dollars. But evidently, many become apathetic.

I watched and waited for Reagan's economics to trickle down for four years. I'm still waiting. In 1988, there was a chance for a more democratic approach. Dissatisfied because I was not "better off than I was four years before," I eagerly cast my second presidential vote. I had transferred to the University in Duluth that fall and immediately registered to vote. Idealism, especially in youth, exceeds pragmatism. I supported Jesse Jackson in the primaries. It was a long shot in a country that would not elect a black president for another twenty years, but I was an idealistic twenty-three-year-old, and Jackson's past relationship with Martin Luther King appealed to me.

Reverend Jackson showed up to speak on the UMD campus that summer. I attended with a friend. Perhaps as an omen, his candidate, Pat Robertson—the old PTL pitchman himself—was also on-site at UMD.

In the spirit of reciprocation, which ideally washes the other hand of friendship, I went with him and heard the rote Christian stump speech. Jackson did quite well in the primary for a black man in 1988, marginally better than a black woman had sixteen years before. He finished second among five other white men, all of whom held elected office.

1988 Democratic Presidential Primaries

Candidate	Delegate count	Popular vote / %	Contests won
Michael Dukakis	1792	10,024,101/42.4	30
Jesse Jackson	1023	6,941,816/29.4	13
Al Gore	374	3,190,992/13.5	7
Paul Simon	161	1,107,692/4.7	1
Dick Gephardt	137	1,452,331/6.1	3

Robertson, who had finished second in the Iowa caucuses, finished poorly in the New Hampshire contest. With his campaign terminated, he urged his supporters to get behind former Vice President George H. W. Bush. Considered the front-runner in October 1987, Bush entered the Republican primary race.

1988 Republican Presidential Primaries

Candidate	Popular vote / %	Contests won
George H. W. Bush	8,235,512/67.9	42
Bob Dole	2,333,375/19.2	5
Pat Robertson	1,097,446/9.0	4

In my youth, I had foreseen a future in which real democracy could take root. I was infatuated with the notion that anything is possible in America. I grew up around the proposition that, despite all its contrived clout, its military spending and bragging rights, the future of America deserved my unbiased vote.

Consider the volatile 1968 election. It was not inconceivable that McCarthy could have won the Democratic nomination. Had a series of events that ended with the assassination of RFK transpired differently, McCarthy might have won. Then, in the end, there was Nixon, the saboteur. On October 31, while I was out collecting for UNICEF, President Johnson went on the air to layout an end game for Vietnam. The president announced that the bombing over North Vietnam, which had been going on since 1965, would be halted, a surprising announcement for which quadrennial Octobers are known. Every treat, though, solicits a trick. People went to bed with visions of peace in their minds. All interested parties were set to gather in Paris to talk about peace. The war ending then, right before the election, was bad for Nixon. All that summer, the Republican candidate, adamant to be president after losing in 1960 by a thin margin to JFK, had been running a covert operation with South Vietnam. He convinced President Thieu to hold out for a better deal than Johnson could give him. The newspaper headlines of November 2 conveyed the message that the war would go on as planned. It was treason which, if leaked, would have surely sunk Nixon. Humphrey would have won, and our involvement in Southeast Asia would have been spared at least three years, billions of dollars, and thousands of lives. Johnson, however, after much deliberation, opted not to make the treasonous act public knowledge. He, defense secretary (succeeding McNamara) Clark Clifford and his staff felt the revelation was too much for the country to handle. Besides, doing so would also reveal the nefarious way the knowledge was obtained.

* * *

That's the deal, and insanity is doing the same thing and expecting different results. In America, you vote your conscience and hope the rest of the majority is as sane—or insane—as you. I sometimes wonder if the GOP guidelines include an insanity clause. Every voting age person should vote for the candidate that thrills them now, that stands above the rest, that can do the best job, and will be judicious in the way they compromise themselves. It is a vote for who can best address the current needs of a nation. Often it is not the front-runner, and if enough vote for the second-place man or woman, or the underdog, in the primary election, by the general election, they may be the front-runner. Traces of democracy easily get lost in America. They can be found just as easily, even maintained, every two years—if the voting age population (VAP) participates in its optimal capacity. History indicates that it has not in elections dating to 1792. For much of the 1800s, the VAP turnout was in the 60 to 70 percent range. Around 1912 when the populist party, socialist and third-party hopefuls started to gather moss, the turnout in presidential elections dropped into the 50 percent range and has rarely risen above it.

I. Welcome to America

One of the penalties for refusing to participate in politics is that you end up being governed by your inferiors.

—Plato

A liberally inclined American will argue that they live in a democracy. More likely, they'll describe, in frustratingly trite detail, a government that desperately and perpetually requires work. The Egalitarian model refers to "A system of government by the whole population." Words that form on the tip of the tongue, at the front of the brain, echoing like a train of thought fighting to stay its course. The many contours to democracy stick like shivs in the sides of a plurality of America, while enough to win elections—and hold America ransom—foster the belief, the intuitively convoluted spirit, that America is a republic. School children are led like sheep, like an obsequious chorus, to ingest this idea and pledge daily "to the republic for which it {the American flag, Trump's cloth surrogate} stands..." They are the "elementary penguins" in "I am the Walrus." A republic also conjures a governmental model, a sovereign state, requiring far less maintenance, in which the people rule. But there is also the implication of supreme power going to a president. The idea is gentrified, modernized from the idea of "a group with a certain equality between its members." For the record, I can't recall pledging to that. If I ever did, I likely had my fingers crossed with the assurance that we can do better.

America is its own reward. Democracy is there for the fight. It's an opportunist's paradise! It is a place where things can happen that could not anywhere else on the globe. Sounds like a sales pitch to me. Yes, rags to riches stories are a dime a dozen here, in the land of majestic purple mountains from the tops of which Martin Luther King could see the "promised land." That implicit contract, the elusive prize in America, swings on a pendulum, a high hung fruit becoming exponentially lower to be reaped by all in the first governmental model. The caveat here is, of course, that everyone eligible exercises their right to vote. We do not have the corner market, though, on freedom. There are other Western European countries, democracies that have free, even direct, elections. Most are better at sending every citizen the message that they and their vote matters, and I'm left wondering how America got such a great reputation. In the elections of 2014 and 2015, Sweden had an 82 percent VAP turnout. America has not hit the 80-percent mark in decades. From 1960 to 1995, Australia and Belgium had the highest voter turnout in the world at 95 percent.

Opportunities may even come to fruition easier in those countries. I have never subscribed to the book of America. The book wasn't written here in 1620 by a coterie of Mayflower miscreants whose descendants would stare at the blue blood in their veins. Perhaps the difference is that there was never a king in America (yet). We have a constitution, yet we don't feel compelled to humor a monarchy, even as in the United Kingdom, seeking Her Majesty's approval on legislation as a formality. Our queen, our figurehead, is in New York Harbor. Norway ranks first as a "full" democracy. In ten countries that have democratic governments, the mighty USA did not even make the list. There is no middleman (or woman) in a full democracy; no constituted college through which the popular vote is diluted, making it accessible to partisan influence. Citizens directly vote on who makes the decisions that affect their lives. People directly vote on whom they want to lead for the respective tenure. America has never tried such a lassie-fare system of governance. There appears to be a fear of electing a president without a net, without the training wheels of the passively presented Madisonian Electoral College. The Civil War ended slavery, one of the fundamental reasons behind the college. In contemporary politics, it acts only as a funnel, a sieve, a channel for votes to go through. It is a safeguard, an insurance plan for those whose blood is blue to have a last-ditch effort for their candidate to win, thereby maintaining their half-nelson, their passive/ aggressive, patronizing hold on America's throttled neck. Twice in modern history, the college has provided a pathway to victory. In either case, the man elected irrevocably damaged the office of the presidency, our international standing, or simply codified the pieces necessary to lead a future of constant fighting for a fair shake for the "popular" part of America. Madison's thought process for the Electoral College included some assurance that a tyrant would not be elected president.

America operates a limited democracy, flawed, and at best, trying to act as a fair compromise between a democracy and something that has most recently resembled a dictatorial monarchy. It is prone to infrequent and varnished splashes bordering on an oligarchy. A factor, which begs consideration, is that Norway is a country of 5.2 million (2017) while the United States deals with 327 million in a much more heterogeneous population. Many of the Scandinavian countries, those in the European Union, have done much better than America as democracies considering their age and previous monarchical systems. A ranking of the ten highest full democracies reveals:

Countries with Unlimited Democracy

Country	Ranking in 10
Norway	9.93
Sweden	9.73
Iceland	9.65
Denmark	9.38
New Zealand	9.26
Australia	9.13
Switzerland	9.09
Canada	9.08
Finland	9.03
Luxembourg	8.8

Nothing is 100 percent, least of all democracy. The idea that any group of humans can hear from EVERYONE equally, honoring the needs of those who are bound to fall through the cracks (or be on crack), has proven to be preposterous, much too great an expectation of America. The opening phrase of our Constitution, "We the people," now stands as a sales pitch, a catch-phrase, something that has admittedly inspired millions to seize opportunity and perpetually work for change, but also is the greatest, the most cogent and copiously heeded lie ever documented. There will always remain even the narrowest of margins that will exceed the democratic citizen's grasp. But, as demonstrated by this handful of precocious countries, voter participation ensures the closest way to that perfect score. Norway ranks 119th in the world in terms of population at 5,353,363. It has not been a homogeneous country for decades, with Somalis, Turks, Moroccans, Africans, Palestinians, to name a few, filling out minorities in large cities like Oslo. In 1984 I went to Norway with a group of mostly Scandinavians. They blended right in. As a biracial person, I was quite conspicuous in a group photo. I do not recall seeing anyone of color, or anyone with black hair for that matter. I guess that sacred Norse-Germanic blood Der Fuhrer once tried to tap does not flow with such stringency anymore. An estimated 88,764 people in Norway are first- or second-generation Africans. Why a Norwegian would want to come to the US, I can't imagine. Perhaps the reason is for the gross negligence in government, for America's perpetual, perhaps impractical, exercise to make it to the list of the ten full democracies. Maybe they want to dream with us, to be part of the never-ending story of America. It is worth noting that all those countries have at least a century on America, and the moss between the cracks reveals time they've had to perfect a governance. Most keep a monarch involved (if heeded at all) as a constant real-time reminder of what they could easily revert to without sufficient participation. Eighty-three percent of Norway is white. They are 100 percent Norwegian. Another 8 percent is from, or has ancestors from, Europe. President Trump outlined, in colorful language, countries from which immigrants are not welcome. He then spoke of the Norwegians he will welcome. I fondly await the arrival of that WASP ship of LGBTQ immigrants from Norway to be welcomed by Mike Pence.

Despite itself, of slavery, of lynching, of Jim Crow, of antisemitism, of "No Irish need apply," of Japanese internment camps... Despite the marginalization and discrimination of nearly every ethnic group to pass through Ellis Island, America somehow acquired this great reputation as a beacon of freedom and democracy. After turning a ship away in 1939 sending hundreds of Jews to a waiting death in Nazi Germany; after dropping chemical weapons continuously on a nation for three years, Central Americans escaping violence in their own country—only to experience violence here—still believe America has a reputation for compassion. Good for them. I applaud their resolve and insistence on finding the best in Americans, which has made a stark appearance of late. I suppose that in comparison, America might look a lot more compassionate. Anyone familiar with past contemporary history should not come to that conclusion. America's past is horrific. When you think about it, heinous unforgivable acts were carried out with a disturbing acceptance in the UNITED STATES of AMERICA. A country founded by puritans, pious Christians who espoused the message of "love thy neighbor." People, pretty much everyone except wealthy white men, were treated atrociously, from African Americans, to Native Americans, to women, to the disabled. The difference is hope, the hint of a chance, influences of enfranchising democracy. In America, one is allowed a dream. People are encouraged to dream by the green woman standing in New York harbor, and the odds are that they will come to fruition. All those horrific things changed. The positive weight that change holds is on a pendulum, getting marginally better, marginally worse...better, worse...never settling. This is the experiment, it's physical laws, how long the weight of that pendulum will continue to sustain movement. It stops if another four years of Trump is allowed.

The treatment of African Americans significantly improved in 200 years, but the better is always available. In America, traditionally, uniquely, that significance is tenuous. It is subject to lapses of equally significant proportion. For the disabled, living conditions and the way they're accepted in society has greatly improved. It is a place where, even over decades, even centuries, dreams could come true. Situations could get better along the way. African Americans went from being enslaved for more than two centuries in this country to holding public office by the end of the nineteenth century. For black men and women, the opportunities to participate in government got progressively better. As a boy, born in the 48th state of the union, Barack Obama set his sights on being president. He did it, fulfilling his goal and the goal of many Americans. That could not have happened in Russia, Saudi Arabia, or North Korea, countries whose methods of governing are embraced by Trump. Those countries are either run by political strongmen who routinely rig elections in their own favor, or are dynasties passed down from generation to generation. The Constitution protects freedom of speech and assembly. It secures a right to protest, to flagrantly contradict government or whoever is leading it. In Russia, that is risky. In Saudi Arabia, contradiction, even from an American, will get you killed for sure. If an immigrant looks past the "Night of Terror" women endured in 1917 in pursuit of voting rights, past the police riot at the 1968 Democratic National Convention, past Kent State; if they ignored, or were even aware of all the police brutality in America's history, they will conclude that in theory, it is a democracy and the law enforcers will ultimately be held accountable and justice will be served. Theoretically, and BTE (before Trump era), a negotiable expectation.

A Vagrant's Tale

In 1988, as a disabled biracial traveler, I determined to go to a remote part of Scotland. I wanted to go off the beaten path, to board the ferry less waked. I went from Larges to Milpo in the Inner Hebrides. There, in my wandering lust to experience the island's remoteness, I was questioned by an off-duty member of Scotland Yard, brought in for questioning as to my purpose, tagged for the color of my skin (possibly awkward gait), I instinctually became impudent. I, too, took my freedoms and civil rights that I have in America for granted. I was in Scotland, and later learned I could have been detained indefinitely, brutalized, and no laws would protect me.

* * *

America is not lawless. We supposedly value life (especially the political pawnage of an unborn one) more than some Central American countries. In Honduras, El Salvador or Guatemala, people fear for their lives daily because of gangs and drug cartels. In some cases, a country's police share its peoples' fear. Honduras ranked number one in homicides for many years, topping out in 2011 with over 91 per every 1,000,000 heads. El Salvador ranks as the most violent country worldwide. It's an unmitigated disaster, a culmination of historic errors. America has a direct correlation to that violence. In 1980 Ronald Reagan was spending billions on El Salvador. He was— with ulterior motives—supplying arms to the Contra rebels to fight the Sandinista government in Nicaragua. Honduras did not have a civil war of its own but served as a staging ground for the US-backed Contra's fight in Nicaragua. The war Reagan proliferated, the tension he exacerbated, in El Salvador between 1979 and 1992, left as many as 75,000 dead. In 1954 the US had signed a treaty with Honduras, vowing to lend military aid to strengthen their army. In the era of Joe McCarthy, and subsequent actions that led to the Vietnam War, the aid was in the spirit of anti-communism. Hey, what's more American than being anti-communist? In Guatemala, the economic and social climate was exacerbated in the 1950s when, in defense of the corporate interests of a fruit company, America helped to depose the Democratic government of Jacob Arbenz Guzmán.

America forages countries for motives. It looks for reasons to start wars and then scrambles to find ways to justify being there. It usually ends up on a courtroom floor with lawyers ferreting out the truth from high-ranking military. For decades America has created conflict wrapped up to look like a proactive endeavor, scuttling bombs wrapped prophylactically to represent the country's current best interest. Usually, though, for America, it is an investment in the future of that country, for better or worse, richer, or poorer. The violence in Central America sure paid off for Donald Trump. It gave him a platform to reach his core supporters. It provided him a vital and mounting need to build a wall on the southern border to stem the tide pool of "murderers and rapists."

El Salvador, Guatemala and Honduras are referred to as the Northern Triangle, countries of a mass exodus. In recent years, tens of thousands, many of them unaccompanied minors, have fled the political corruption. They are escaping a situation that leaves them the choice of joining a gang or being killed. Women are faced with being a drug mule or being raped and killed. In America, the migrants sit—since 2017 not immune to physical and sexual violation—in a detention center, or camp (if they make it that far), slowly going through a legal system which makes America what it is, or was; a comparably compassionate and judicial country. They come here seeking asylum, and they are either deported or detained for indefinite periods of time. In 2015, the number of refugees from the Northern Triangle reached 110,000, five times the number three years earlier. When asked why they seek asylum, migrants cite violence, forced gang recruitment and extortion (countries pay millions annually in fees). The homicide rate in El Salvador is 103 per thousand. It has decreased marginally in recent years, but the violence in the Northern Triangle is still significantly higher than Belize, Costa Rica, Nicaragua or Panama. Extortion is omnipresent. In 2015 a Honduran newspaper estimated that in total, the Northern Triangle countries pay over 600 million in annual extortion fees to organized crime groups. The causes of the violence stem from the decades of war in the countries of the Triangle, much of which is homegrown in America.

Violence spreads like wildfire in unstable nations, nations that might not be democratic at the time, or those that have never known democracy and are resistant to it. US forces were the proxies for South Vietnam. For roughly thirteen years, they and their allies fought an enemy that ultimately questioned to whom it was loyal. Prior to that, for at least fifteen years, the US provided either military or financial aid to "free Vietnam." We aided the French who were fighting the Chinese Communists. The US has intervened disastrously in the Middle East. In 1978 President Carter brought the countries of Israel and Egypt to a peace agreement. In contemporary history, Carter stands out as a president who did nothing to intentionally stoke the cauldron of world violence. If he did, in the case of Iran, it was a result of his sense of ethics, a refusal to not extradite the Shah to go back to Iran where he would most likely be executed following a trial. Surely Carter had nothing to gain by his action. On the contrary, fifty-two American hostages were taken and remained in Iran until January 20, 1981, and were released moments after Ronald Reagan took the Oath of Office. America deconstructs the world a good deal of the time. Look at the Middle East two decades into the twenty-first century, and things look pretty much the same, only much worse. Don't worry. Trump's son-in-law, whose only qualification may be that he wears a yarmulka, is on it.

The actions one president takes has repercussions for the next— or the next. FDR turns away a ship full of Jewish refugees (the same one Canada repelled), he detains Japanese Americans, and history overshadows it because of all the other lasting good he did for America. Truman drops the atomic bomb on two Japanese cities, a calculated move to end WWII, to bring the win-or-die Japanese to surrender. Eisenhower first sends military advisors to Vietnam. In September 1954, the US formed the Southeast Asia Treaty Organization (SEATO) with Great Britain, France, Australia, New Zealand, the Philippines, Pakistan and Thailand. An earlier Geneva Agreement had specified that Vietnam, Cambodia or Laos would not join any other international military alliance. Kennedy sends more advisors and subsequently hid the fact that he was sending 400 special forces soldiers to Vietnam. Until the spring of 1965, Johnson tried to keep US involvement to the level of his predecessors. By 1967 opponents to the war were asking him, "how many kids did you kill today." A cartoon of the time had him seated as a defendant with McNamara and Rusk (Secretary of State) with Nazi war criminals at Nuremberg. In January 1969, Nixon augmented the war's intensity, attacking a North Vietnamese supply line in Cambodia. Each president propelled the lie into epic, almost negligible, proportions. The 1974 midterm election added forty-nine seats to Democrats' favor in the House, surpassing a two-thirds majority. In the Senate, they came out with a sixty to thirty-eight split in their favor. As promised, Nixon had pulled out most of our troops from Vietnam in 1973. Hostilities rose, the war continued, and the new Democratic hold in Congress was a factor in the Viet Cong capturing Saigon in the spring of 1975. The new Democratic-controlled Congress wisely did not appropriate funds for a futile war.

From Madison (War of 1812) to Bush Jr. (second Iraq War), the record for American presidents starting serial wars is not good. They try to disguise ulterior motives sometimes in necessary war paint. For the brunt of modern history, our presidents have had corrupt intentions. And America quite carelessly proliferates around the world, selling itself and its brand of democracy to nations who, in many cases, have leaders to whom the idea of a democratic government is inconceivable, who have for generations complacently conducted a dictatorship. America leaves—or doesn't—their calling card like a Florida swampland salesman. No manufacturer's warranty. If a country tries a democracy and it doesn't work, leaving the country to descend into endless civil war, America is gone. Carpetbaggers run, and a handful of troops are left indefinitely to "teach" what America has forever failed. US forces are now in Iraq fighting "ISIS terrorist gangs," according to CNN. They are in Afghanistan with no exit plan, and history repeats itself. One is an exception to a precedent that was becoming boilerplate, but America is taking responsibility. Bush was spoiling for a war in Iraq, to win where "poppy" Bush had lost. His son went in illegally, without an adequate coalition, destabilizing an already precarious situation, and created a vacuum for networks of terrorist cells like Al-Qaeda, a conglomerate of Islamic extremists and Salafist Jihadists. Bush destabilized Iraq with his pre-emptive invasion, an impulsive action motivated by greed and nepotism that had repercussions on the stability of the region. Syria, in 2018, was occupied by 500 US troops. On the border of Iraq, Bashar al-Assad feared the uprising of his people on whom he is rumored to have used chemical weapons. The US and Russia occupied Syria. America was "led" by a man who lacked any capacity for genuine empathy or sympathy for any situation that, at some point, won't benefit him. On the morning of April 17, 2017, on Trump's command, the US Navy launched fifty-nine Tomahawk cruise missiles at Syria from ships in the Mediterranean Sea. Destabilization in the region has spread to Yemen's civil war, where US intervention is causing massive death and imminent starvation of children.

A part of America is mean-spirited. There is no way around it. It is veiled by things like religion and its timeless cling to democracy. It is a real part that refuses to die, won't realize their sick and reprehensible tendencies; it is a part that will never just shrivel up and go away. Jut as eugenics, or even ethnic cleansing, fails in the end, so too will eradicating the "bad gene" part of America carries. History tells of Democrats and Republicans who have done the wrong thing at the wrong time. America has been as fallible to inhumanity as the most insentient countries on earth, although the incidents are isolated and not commonplace—relatively speaking. So, the question I ask is why, then, would a refugee opt for America rather than one of the top "full" democracies like Sweden, Finland or Norway. Is it, in the 2018 situation on the Southern border, a matter of logistics? I suppose. Geographically, America is the most accessible democratic nation. According to reports by Hondurans to the Norwegian Refugee Council, many who fled the Northern Triangle had no real preference of where their journey ended. They sought safety, self-sufficiency and the right to work. Many were willing to relocate as far as Asia. So, America remains as the most accessible, feasible beacon of democracy. We have established that it is far from a perfect one, its progressive value greatly depreciated by the Trump administration. The recorded black marks of his corrupting predecessors are obliterated by comparison. Yet despite all the isolated incidents of discriminatory policy in the last three centuries, the inhuman treatment of involuntary African migrants before that, the less than warm welcome of almost every group to come here, the military damage done to other countries to which the US turns its back at the fallout, the numerous injustices still existing in the twenty-first century, people have a nagging need or desire to come here. Ideally, they want to come here to become a citizen and vote, and theoretically have a say in the government that was founded on the proposition of one man one vote. They intend, they dream, being witnesses to the precedence of success or failure, to build on that proposition. They hope to someday participate in what stands—in writing—as a government of, by, and for the people.

In many ways, America is a commercial, propagandized to the world. It presents itself (most administrations) as a fair but tough ally, a negotiator, a militaristic strongman with no apparent motive. There is no denying that America is a land of opportunity, that is an affirmation, an action required to live up to the name. That might be America's greatest selling point—an ability to legislate a somewhat equal opportunity for all regardless of gender, race, religion or ability. America makes a livable democracy despite itself. Like Icarus, America rises and often flies too close to the sun. Wings melt despite their span, their tenacious efforts to avoid the pitfalls and landmines of human suffrage. Contemporaneously, America grows ever closer to the sun, with practically every state government agreeing on climate change. On June 1, 2017, Donald Trump renounced America's participation in the 2015 Paris Climate Change Mitigation, making it the only country in the world not involved. Yet sixty-five percent of Americans feel it is important to keep green, to significantly reduce carbon emissions by 2050.

America has a way of setting an example for the world or is at least often looked to for doing so. America rises to challenges that do (or don't potentially) affect the world. From getting in—only after Germany and Italy declared war on it December 11, 1941—WWII to stop Hitler and his assault on a continent and a genocide, to efforts by others outside the government—like 80s aid concerts—to stop hunger in Africa, America has proved its compassionate, humanitarian, and evidently altruistic efforts. But there is that constant incongruence, the plethora of historical infractions that paint America as anything but compassionate. With notable exceptions (FDR, LBJ) those infractions have been the work of Republicans who comprise 24 percent (Gallup, 2017) of America. Independents tend to be more democratic, apt to vote against illegal wars and bills that result in refugees seeking asylum being sent back to the violence they left. They poll at 41 percent, leaving 31 percentage points to the Democrats. The case to be made for coming here, and being treated fairly and humanely, is stronger. The odds are in an immigrant's favor. Try telling that to a refugee detained at the southern border. Evidently, the democratic ethos this country elicits, strains each decade to survive, was even stronger during the Trump years. It's an equation of suppression. Physics. The harder Republicans try to snuff out democracy, take minority rights away, turn America into an exclusive club, the harder Democrats fight to keep the melting pot open. For every action, there is an opposing reaction, binary poles shifting, drifting in their proximal nature until they pass each other.

In the 2016 election, Democrats won the popular vote. It would, regardless of the Electoral College, stand as a true measure of the consensus in America. In 2012 Barack Obama defeated Mitt Romney in both popular and electoral votes. The same thing had happened with McCain four years earlier. John Kerry lost to George W. Bush in 2004 by 3,021,166 votes or 2.4 percent. As was the case in 2004, I think it is safe to say that Bush's handling of the 9/11 terrorist attacks had much to do with his winning margin of popularity. In 2000 Al Gore won the popular vote by a slight margin (543,895), but enough to make it clear that democracy was the popular choice. It was enough to show, at the first presidential contest of the twenty-first century, that the Electoral College is antiquated and does not allow the best, or even most popular, man or woman to win. The last five elections in a new century (after the re-aligning one in 1968) stand as proof that America wants to be a full democracy. History has proven that the majority of people want one.

Build it, and they will come. Can that philosophy be applied to a democracy? Does one have to be a political scientist to fundamentally understand the word, the means of organizing a populace? Imagine if you will that Trump killed the elephant in the room, that in the post-Trump world, the Republican Party ceased to exist, at least in a form that earned it the name Grand Old Party. America would be democratic, no division of vision. Or would it? What about the Libertarians, the

Greens, the Constitution Party, and all the splintering parties who feel America should be raised in different ways? They are all there on the ballot (in some states) in presidential elections. Through the mid-1800s, there were additional parties—the Whigs, the Know Nothings—whose candidates succeeded. For more than a century, it's been Democrats or Republicans winning federal elections. Occasionally a third party wins at the state level (Reform Party candidate Jesse Ventura was governor in Minnesota from 1999 to 2003).

In 1968 there was a splintering of the Democratic Party. Motivated by sentiment to end the Vietnam War, the assassination of Robert Kennedy and Martin Luther King Jr., the withdrawal of Johnson from the presidential race, the party was bifurcated. It was as tribal in its allegiances and ideals as Trump has made the Republican Party. In 2020, after a prodigiously guilty president was acquitted in a partisan vote, and long before, the GOP lies in dire need of repair.

The calculus of the American elections all too infrequently allows for a third party to get on the ballot, to, at best, sell their wares, introduce ideas with the hope they will catch on enough to make a difference. Although they often serve as a decoy, attracting votes destined for the pocket of the candidate usually proposing ideas regressive in nature. In 2016, Gary Johnson (governor of New Mexico) won enough votes in the primaries to earn a place on the ballot in the general election. Libertarians were credited in that election. They placed, far from winning. They earned a place in the possibly-heard-from-again parties like the Progressives had (for its time) in 1912. The idea Libertarian and Green Party (Jill Stein) voters rely on is that with every placement of their candidate on the ballot, and the ensuing votes from voters who have long since tired of the dichotomy in this country, the more potential a third party has of being a contender. Not just a contender, but an aspirant to be in that esteemed class of major party. Over the course of many election cycles, or even in the unprecedented upset of just one, a third party could actually win enough electoral votes to win. Although America would still not make the top ten list of full democracies. Close, no cigar. At the very least, more people can vote for their candidate to have a shot at how they'd like to see America run.

Late in February 2000, Ralph Nader began his campaign for president on the Green Party ticket. He touted the motive "a crisis of democracy." Nader was the Green Party nominee, the Vermont Progressive Party, and the United Citizens' Party of South Carolina. The forty-three states in which he appeared on the ballot was an increase of twenty-two from his presidential bid four years earlier. In 1996 he won 2.7 percent of the popular vote, but it takes five percent to be eligible for federally distributed public funding for the next election. Nader did, however, succeed in getting the Green Party ballot status. He could have been, if only in a few states, a contender. It flushed the squirreled away voters out, the ones not voting until a certain aspect of American life or issue was prominently addressed.

In the 2000 presidential election, there surfaced a "spoiler." The popular allegation dictated that Nader had caused Gore to lose the race. In Florida, the decisive swing state of the notorious recount, Nader had picked up 97,421 votes, with candidates Pat Buchanan and Harry Brown netting 17,484 and 16,415, respectively. To the victor go the spoils. As the third-party candidate with the most votes, Nader likely still bears the stigma of being the man who took the election from Gore. Thus, there is a purging of America that arrives by trend. It occurs when there is enough pent up anger for government to swing, to resemble more closely a fair, or even full, democracy. When leaders of parties are plucked from the plumage of hats nobly tossed into the political arena that have served to advance the drive toward an equal representation of the American populace, this plucking, this fraternization with a single or dual party system, trends. It stays, it strays, it challenges boundaries. The Prohibition Party is a good example. It saw its trend, had its time and place in history. It had a reason, too, a motivation. Perhaps it was entirely serendipitous, wholly capricious, but it served as a vehicle by which women took their first adamant steps towards equality. Beginning in 1869, the party has had enough members to register as a party with ideals, most of which have lost any political interest over the years.

* * *

Welcome to America! You are expected to vote as soon as you are legally able. Why, you huddled befuddled masses ask? Of course, to perpetuate the legend that it can keep—or lead to—the vetted kind of democracy the better half of the founders saw. Your vote helps keep the US in the running for a spot in the top ten. Vote because you can, more importantly, because people have suffered greatly, even died, to do so. In all likelihood, a naturalized citizen will vote with a passion and consistency that usurps their natural-born American countryman or woman. Until the twenty-first century, one could say elections, as far as global interference, were free and fair. Domestic interference has a much more checkered history. You vote in America and hope for the best, being left with that same hopeful look on the ballot taker's face assuring you that your vote will be counted. You vote in America in every election because of the law of averages.

The Story of a Naturalized Citizen

My adoptive father came to the United States as a child in 1939, fleeing Nazi Germany with his parents. He became a citizen in 1945, almost immediately exercising his rights as one. In 1948 he worked on the campaign of Progressive Henry Wallace, former VP to Roosevelt. As a young adult in the 1960s, he probably knew the electoral process better than most Americans his age. He worked through the system, broken as it is, to improve human rights. He marched for civil rights. In 1968, when Democracy was at a low point (hindsight really is 20/20, trite but oh so true), he worked for Minnesota senator Gene McCarthy. Along with US Congressman Don Fraser, he taught perspective McCarthy voters of the caucus process. Caught up in the political process, he attended the many DFL (Democratic-farmer labor) between the initial local precinct caucus and the Democratic National Convention. I write about his experience as a delegate to that most volatile convention in my book *Ten Years and Change: A Liberal Boyhood in Minnesota*. Having grown up as a child in Germany in the prolific years (1933–1939) to the Holocaust as a Jew under the boot of oppression, in the worst Fascist regime imaginable, the partisan injustice he saw was likely obfuscated. These people had a voice, muted as it was, which was more than he had known.

II. Electoral College

Always vote for principle, though you may vote
alone, and you may cherish the sweetest reflection
that your vote is never lost.

–John Adams

James Madison is remembered, not because his wife rescued a portrait of George Washington as the White House burned, but for his "buffer zone." For its time, the Electoral College was a pragmatic solution for electing a president. It was one of many proposed at the Constitutional Convention. With the historical honorarium "father of the Constitution," Madison was not in favor of our current method of electing a president. In the model we now use, the electoral votes in nearly all states are awarded to the statewide winner of the popular vote. In his post-presidential years, Madison consistently argued for alternatives to the winner-take-all system of choosing a state's presidential electors. At the 1787 convention in Philadelphia, two issues were the subjects of contentious debate; how votes should be counted in small and large states, and how to count free states and slave states. Contrary to what many of its defenders today contend, the college was not created to give smaller states equal representation. It was instead intended to reflect the political realities—of the time—associated with accommodating the institution of slavery into an electoral system. A buffer had to be created. A direct election system in the years of slavery would have put southern states at a distinct disadvantage, as the slaves did not have a vote. They were people, or property at least, things of personal wealth that should count toward something. The issue was raised of how slaves would be counted. This was necessary not only for tax purposes but also in figuring how many seats a state could have in the US House of Representatives for the next ten years. Delegates James Wilson and Roger Sherman proposed a three-fifths compromise. They arrived at this fraction by counting every three out of five slaves as a person designated for this purpose. The intended effect was to give southern states a third more seats in Congress as well as a third more electoral votes (ah, the foundation of the intrinsic upper hand, the smell of baking cake). The compromise gave the states more votes than if the slaves were ignored, but fewer than if slaves and free citizens were counted equally. The system was rigged, fixed to favor slaveholders' interests, at least until 1861. A clause in the Fourteenth Amendment effectively repeals the compromise. Former slaves could vote, on paper, and the African Americans expected to be counted along with white men. Excluded were non-taxpaying Native Americans—one bridge at a time. Toward the end of Reconstruction, former slave states were busy finding loopholes in the new mandates. They made it nearly impossible for African Americans to vote. (It is the same states suppressing the black vote 141 years later in the 2018 midterm election.) All the while, the states were still reaping the benefits of the elections of representatives based on the total population.

In the slave era, states varied in the suffrage rights. Pennsylvania, for example, had fairly liberal rights. Massachusetts did not. Basing an election on a national popular vote tends to convert each state's votes together on an equal basis. This was why delegates from states with limited suffrage opposed a direct election of a president. Madison argued for the national popular vote, however, claiming that "The people at large was the fittest" body to choose an executive. He felt that "local considerations should give way to the general interest." In other words, even though direct elections would put states (such as his own Virginia) at an electoral disadvantage, he, for one, was willing to sacrifice for the good of the democracy they were outlining. Had Madison's fellow

Southerners felt similarly, seen a window to be a political martyr open, the Electoral College might have never been born. In the end, Madison was forced to abandon the idea of directly electing a president. Fathers sometimes need to make compromises too.

In the early nineteenth-century, the concession of direct elections for an Electoral College system began to change. At its inception, each elector was awarded two votes to cast. It was how presidents and vice presidents were chosen. The winner of the most votes was president and winner of the second most got to be vice president. Political parties began forming, and the field of viable candidates from which a voter could choose was numerous. In the 1796 presidential election, the winner, John Adams, was bound by rules he had played a role in making. He was required to take Thomas Jefferson as his vice president, rather than his preferred running mate Charles Pinckney.

Candidates in 1796 Presidential Election

Candidate	Political party	Position
Thomas Jefferson	Democratic-Republican	Former secretary of state
Aaron Burr	Democratic-Republican	US senator (NY)
Samuel Adams	Democratic-Republican	Governor of Massachusetts
George Clinton	Democratic-Republican	Former governor of New York
John Adams	Federalist	Vice president
Thomas Pinckney	Federalist	Former governor of South Carolina
Oliver Ellsworth	Federalist	US Chief Justice
John Jay	Federalist	Governor of New York
James Iredell	Federalist	Assoc. Justice of U.S Supreme Court
Samuel Johnston	Federalist	Former US Senator (NC)
Charles C Pinckney	Federalist	US Minister to France

The incumbent president George Washington decided not to seek a third term in office. The Federalists chose Adams as their candidate with Jefferson gaining support of the Democratic-Republicans. With the limited suffrage available in states, out of just under 4,000,000 people (1790 census) 20.1 percent voted. Only 804,000 people who were eligible voted (a fact that makes not voting today seem petty, having been eclipsed by centuries of democracy).

Presidential Election of 1796

Candidate/ running mate	Home state	Popular vote/ %	Electoral vote	States carried
John Adams/ Thomas Pinckney	Massachusetts	35,725/ 53.	71	9
Thomas Jefferson/ Aaron Burr	Virginia	31,115/ 46.6	68	7

In 1804, the awkward position John Adams was put in by having to accept Thomas Jefferson as his vice president changed. The original rules made no distinction between voting for president and vice president on an electoral basis, making it conceivable that there could be a bi-partisan president and vice president (Lincoln and Andrew Johnson). The framers must not have anticipated the future elections in which multiple parties would contend. By definition, having at least two opposing parties is necessary to be political. The Twelfth Amendment to the Constitution reversed that. Both the presidential elections of 1796 and 1800 were enough impetus for the electoral process to be changed. In June of 1804, the electoral process assumed new guidelines. The amended system required that a contingent election be held by the House of Representatives if no candidate wins a presidential electoral vote from a majority of electors. Also, the number of candidates allowed to be contenders in a contingent election was narrowed from five to three. The Senate then held a contingent election of its own for vice president if no candidate won a majority of the electoral votes for that office. The amendment also stipulated that an individual deemed ineligible—by vote—for president was eligible to be vice president. In most states, to this day, the winner-take-all ruling applies. The winning candidate of a majority, or plurality of the popular vote, takes all the state's electoral votes. (Nebraska and Maine are the only states not to follow this3months before an election, almost as if it were the last tertiary item on a to-do list. One could argue that the appointment, or election, of a vice president in his or her own right may have been better as far as voter turnout if voters knew for months exactly the ticket they were getting. Since 1804, the president and vice president have been elected on separate ballots. Today, a presidential candidate chooses a running mate if for no other reason than to balance the ticket. He or she (in 1984 Geraldine Ferraro was Walter Mondale's pick) is usually of lesser political stature. They usually are less well known or experienced, but still is the person second in line to be president, a factor that could weigh heavily with voters if the presidential candidate was older or in questionable health. Nine times in our history, a vice president has had to ascend to the presidency through death: John Tyler, Millard Fillmore, Andrew Johnson, Chester Arthur, Teddy Roosevelt, Calvin Coolidge, Harry Truman and Lyndon Johnson. In the case of Richard Nixon, Gerald Ford became president through his resignation, making Ford the only man to win both the presidency and vice presidency without winning the popular or electoral vote (Ford became Nixon's vice president in December 1973 after Spiro Agnew resigned amid scandal).

On Friday, August 29, 2008, presidential candidate John McCain introduced Sarah Palin to America, at least the lower 48. She was governor of Alaska but still a much lesser known politician. She was easy on the eyes, younger, but less experienced and reputedly not that bright. That fit well, almost a credential for the job. However, as time went on, nearing the election, journalists discovered that the governor of our forty-ninth state was not well-read, unable to name a newspaper she read. It took exhaustive coaching to prepare her for her one vice presidential debate with incumbent Democrat Joe Biden. Voters reassessed their confidence in the McCain ticket, perhaps favoring previous choices for running mates, including Mitt Romney, Joe Lieberman, Representative Eric Cantor (R-VA) or former Pennsylvania Governor Tom Ridge. Voters undoubtedly questioned whether Palin would be ready to assume the presidency of a man over twenty years her senior. In 2008, McCain was seventy-two and had been diagnosed with melanoma three years earlier. The chances of Palin having to take the role of president, if not that of acting president (such as Bush after the assassination attempt on Reagan), were statistically good. My point is that, as the selection, election and appointment of a vice presidential candidate or running mate has become progressively—since 1804— more of a casual last-thing-on-the-list nature, voters don't know what comes with their candidate. Such a turn of events two months prior to an election may very well influence, disturb or cancel their vote. In McCain's case, it is likely that it cost him the presidency.

* * *

Baked into the cake, the Constitution is the recipe for a much less-than-full democracy. The decision Americans must make when they go to the polls, when they file their taxes, when they are summoned to serve on a jury, is whether they see that democracy as half full or half empty. The Constitution decreed that presidents are elected by states, not people. Since 1804 electors have been selected based on the popular vote of a state's residents, not on what its legislature wanted. So, technically one could claim an individual's input is in there, being considered in the great cognizant political machine, thereby validating America's ever-lasting classification as a limited democracy that I suggest can be seen as half-full or half-empty. We are left with an interminably indirect course to elect a president. In the event of elections that pushed the electoral envelope to the point where the popular vote was lost and a candidate still won, the best hope is that enough electors will renege, be "faithless," to alter the outcome. In 1896 four faithless electors voted at the national meeting of the Electoral College. They ditched their vow to vote for the Peoples' Party to vote for the Democratic Party's vice-presidential candidate, Arthur Sewall.

Twice in fifty-seven presidential elections have multiple electors not voted for their sworn party, a living presidential candidate. In 1808 eight electors did not vote for the party to which they had pledged, their candidate James Madison. The election of 1832 pitted Democrat Andrew Jackson against National Republican Henry Clay. Two avowed National Republicans gave their votes to Jackson. The Electoral College is not impervious to the will of the people. It has been upset, steering the election of a president into more democratic waters. In 1836 Richard M. Johnson earned the distinction of being the only candidate in history to scare up enough faithless electors to push the election out of the Electoral College for Congress to decide. Johnson was on the Democratic ticket that year as the vice-presidential candidate of Martin Van Buren.

In the early days of voting, decades before electing a president was a contest to see which side can pack the most mud into a sling-shot, or who could afford to buy the most TV time, a comparatively small percentage of the VAP took the task of selecting the chief executor of laws for the next four years seriously. Voting was guarded. Slaves and women were not included. Neither were the lower classes that did not own slaves and/or land. And only those over twenty-one could vote. That narrows the field significantly. There were no staged events such as "October surprises" with the sole purpose of maligning an opponent, always executed with a choreographed timing and desperate flare. By any standards of contemporary politics, it was hardly representative, far from being a definitive democracy. The election process was, however, pragmatic and driven by a unifying objective, met with a collective appreciation of what was at stake. Could this systemic disintegration of purpose, of moral fiber, of not focusing on maligning and subsequent investigation and indictment of one's opponent have led to the constant motivation required to get even half of the VAP to vote? It was not a rushed event, the presidential election, and might take place over weeks. The very first election in the new union of states began December 15, 1788 and lasted until January 10, 1789. It sounds like the early voting of today, allowed in twenty-two states and the District of Columbia. In the first election of a president, someone to lead, approve and execute the functions of government, Federalists supported ratification of the Constitution that had been written earlier in the summer of 1788. There was one dissenter, an anti-federalist, who did not support the ratification of the Constitution. That first presidential election had no political parties, just conjecture on how the government would be. No inherent motives, politics to play emblematic of a party. The purposes of election were much less ambiguous, far from the centrifugal circuses most generations voting today know.

The Electoral College, per Article II of the Constitution, supersedes the popular vote and alone can win elections. Each state legislature appoints its electors to the college, comprising 538 members. A presidential candidate must secure an absolute majority of 270 electoral votes to win. In 1788 there were sixty-nine electoral votes at stake, and a candidate needed thirty-five of them to win. Given the number of people who could not vote then, it is not surprising that only 11.6 percent voted in the 1788 election. The weak turnout in the first election was rigged. The meek, in this case, inherit nothing but a stem in which the playing field was interminably tilted to give the upper class an upper hand. The sloth at the polls wasn't a result of lack of interest; it was mired in voter status. Educated white men of age and means voted, reducing the participation to a mere fraction of the total population of thirteen states. No official laws existed to outright ban "immigrants" from voting. However, they were greatly discouraged, becoming the recipients of constant anti-immigrant rhetoric.

1896 Presidential Election

Candidate	Running mate	Party	Alliance	Popular vote / %	Elect. vote
William McKinley	Garret Hobart	Republican		7,111,607/ 51.0	271
William Jennings Bryan	Arthur Sewall Thomas Wattson	Democratic	Democratic Silver, Populist	6,509,052/ 46.7	176

It was a realigning election, a campaign that had taken place during the "Panic of 1893." Between 1893 and 1897, a serious economic depression affected every component of the economy, resulting in the election of William McKinley. It also shaped politics, tempered how and when people vote, ended the old third-party system (1854–1895) and gave rise to a fourth party system (1896–1932). At the 1896 Democratic National Convention in Chicago, in five ballots, Sewall was the unanimous choice for vice-presidential nominee. An alliance was formed with the populists who had chosen Bryan as their presidential nominee. In a show of solidarity, distancing themselves from the Democrats, the Populists insisted on Georgia Representative Thomas Wattson as their vice-presidential nominee. Incumbent president Grover Cleveland was denounced, and Bryan was nominated by the Democrats as well as the Populists. He was opposed by some more conservative "Bourbon" Democrats who formed the National Democratic Party and nominated their candidate, John M. Palmer.

The country was reacting to growth, to politics stimulated by business and global interests. Many of the planks in the Democrat's 1896 platform concerned money—the printing, minting and distribution of it. Tariffs were of concern, as was immigration. Former Ohio Governor William McKinley won the Republican nomination on the first ballot, with Garret Hobart as vice-presidential nominee. Their platform called for the acquisition of Hawaii and sections of Denmark's West Indies. It favored women's rights and introduced the idea of equal pay. The Republicans also pushed for the exclusion of illiterate immigrants. They had a vested interest in expanding the US, the motive being increasing the electoral base. The platform introduced at the convention that year also proposed that a canal be dug through Central America, linking the Pacific and Atlantic Oceans. Much like the oceans, parties were parting while also merging. The third or fourth party may present more options for the voter, but within the confines of the Electoral College, it can change a state's winner in one such state by gaining enough votes that would otherwise have gone to a major party. If a presidential election has equally close numbers, a third party may determine the outcome of an election by winning only a small percentage of the vote. Conversely, in a winner-take-all system, there is nothing gained by the second-place candidate. The effect is that two parties usually dominate plurality electoral systems unfavorably to third or fourth parties. This pattern of the electoral process follows what political scientists term Duverger's law. The theory proposes that plurality-rule elections, at any stage, predicated on a single-member district, tend to favor a two-party system. Maurice Duverger, a French sociologist, claimed that there existed two paths whereby a plurality voting system can lead to fewer major parties. He claimed there was a "fusion," an alliance of weaker parties morphing into more effective sub-groups. Gradually, the weaker parties dissolve, voters desert them, concluding they can neither win nor significantly influence government. Congressional districts then act as a catalyst, awarding only the winner in each a seat. The party to come in second, or third, place successively in every district will not gain seats in the House of Representatives, even if they win a sizable minority of votes. In terms of geography, parties that are sparsely spread are at a virtual disadvantage. Densely concentrated parties, which get the same public support and recognition, are in a better position.

On November 5, 1996, 8.7 percent of the voting-age population voted for Reform candidate Ross Perot. His opposing major party candidates, Bill Clinton and Bob Dole, won 49.2 and 40.7 percent of the vote, respectively. Perot, who had run as an Independent four years earlier and won 18.9 percent of the popular vote, was excluded from the 1996 presidential debates. He was a billionaire businessman who talked excessively and comically about "cleaning out the barn," getting rid of "pork-barrel" projects in Washington, cutting waste in government and generally lowering the national debt. He was concerned about attention given to POW/MIA veterans left in Southeast Asia. Fair, important, equitable causes to some, but it was from a third-party candidate. American politics may well be a victim of its own system, a pot melted for the supplanting of pigeon-holes, learned over centuries, normalized enough so the plurality will always vote Democrat or Republican. From its beginning, the Electoral College was considered a fundamental, "baked in the cake," ingredient to the macrocosmic federal plan. Many oppose it, find it falsely representative and antiquated. But just as the concept demonstrates, the true will of the people is missed. It would take a constitutional amendment to get rid of it, which is unlikely to happen. The requisite three-fourths (thirty-eight states) would have to include one or two southern states, most of whom wanted the system in the first place. But were that to happen soon, given the apparent democratic trend, voters may not necessarily be satisfied with the result. Campaigns have long been based on winning electoral votes. Every election night, we monitor the television anxiously for that magic 270, a number indelibly lodged in any politically-minded voter's brain. Who will get their first is truthfully all we care about. For my generation, the lesson was taught in 2000 that the popular vote is just a number that, in the end, is ostensibly insignificant. One votes in the primary for whomever they want. That may provide to electors a general idea of what each party is thinking, which candidate is popular, before the party convenes to choose their nominee. In 2016, I voted for Sanders in the primary. It turned out that Hillary Clinton was 12.1 percent more popular. She had amassed 977 more delegate votes than Sanders. The Democrat's nominated Clinton. So, one can either write in a candidate or, in that case, vote Libertarian or Green. Each option is ultimately detracting from Clinton's electoral vote count and serving them on a platter to Trump.

The candidate that loses is quantified. Pollsters pour over how hard a candidate campaigned, how much they spent on advertising, and when and where it was. In the final analysis, they may choose to blame the system, saying it is rigged, a common (and theoretically founded) accusation made in an Electoral College winner-take-all system. You can only fool some of the people some of the time. In 2016 Trump even said that Sanders had gotten a raw deal, how it was rigged with super delegates. This from a man who'd claim any race was rigged that didn't end with him winning. He knew Clinton, with all her baggage, Benghazi, Whitewater, Bill, and a woman, who was likely easier to beat in the general election. Imagine a system based on the popular vote, where the size of a state cannot affect the fairness of an election or an individual's participation in a democracy. In a lesser sense, campaigns could still gravitate toward gaining the popular vote. One party's candidate will win, one will lose, and (as Bob Dylan wrote) the loser now will be later to win—because it's a truly democratic system now. Critics will still tend to look at where a candidate campaigned, how much they spent on advertising and when and where it was. In the end, the loser will still say things were rigged. They might even challenge the very system they wanted, amended the US Constitution to get, and we are back where we began. It could happen, and as history consistently proves, its often the Republicans who are the sore losers and will blame a system long before admitting that they simply have a bad candidate who, in Trump's case, only wants to sow divisiveness and can't even pretend to lead the people in any measure that could be remotely seen as proactive.

There are pros and cons of a system that virtually ensures that one of two parties will win. The presidents who have won by electoral votes alone can be counted on one hand. Still, it is the principle, the point that there exists a way to circumvent the real, direct, Jeffersonian "one man, one vote" process. Each presidential year some voter will bring forth a resolution to abolish the Electoral College. It remains because:

1. It protects minority interests, preserving the voice of states with lower populations and those of rural areas, known red hat/neck breeding grounds. They are the Tea-partiers who elected Trump.

2. It nurtures a two-party system. The fact is, according to the *Asia-Pacific Economic Blog*, is that the Democrat-Republican dichotomy adds stability.

3. It delivers more power to the states. By giving states power to elect their own delegates to the Electoral College, a representative government is furthered (according to the *US Election Atlas*).

There are as many arguments against the college. Yes, it does function fundamentally to protect the minorities and under-represented groups in rural America (i.e., Trumpers) who have a right to be heard from with equal respect. It also, as 2016 proved, opens the door to any half-baked, hostile, maliciously inclined, inexperienced candidate to run as a populist. Even when the ideas the candidate espouses are in opposition to the other two-thirds of the country, ideas that are odorous even to the voters who "held their nose" to vote for Trump. In his case, the choice of candidate was intentional, deliberate, selected for the sole function of "shaking up the system." That they did. And for four years, god forbid eight, the nation and the world suffer. The Electoral College should either be repealed or reformed for that reason which has allowed a madman to rip democracy to shreds and others that include:

- The candidate chosen by a majority of Americans may not win. Many think it is undemocratic that some smaller states have a larger percentage of electoral votes despite their low population in the US.

- It adds complexity to an essentially simple process of your candidate winning, of having your vote tallied, based on a popular vote. In the end, the added bell and dog-whistle may incline a voter not to play at all.

- Small and swing states are given more power. A large, populous state like California, with fifty-five electoral votes, indicates that there are 705,405 people per vote. In stark contrast, in Wyoming, holding a mere three electoral votes, there are 194,717 people per vote. The idea of "one man one vote" is lost, impossible, implausible within the confines of the college.

The reasons to keep it around find balance with those to dump it. They are rendered and balance equally, which is more than we can say for the process America agitatedly accepts for election fare. The Electoral College will likely be a standard in American politics for at least another decade of election cycles. That is hopeful, nearsightedly optimistic in response to what happened in 2016. The truth is that it is unlikely that the Electoral College is going anywhere. Towards the end of her senatorial career, Barbara Boxer (D-CA) introduced legislation to get rid of the college. It came soon after Hillary Clinton won 2,850,961 more popular votes and still lost the 2016 presidential race by the college upset. Trump won the electoral vote by seventy-four votes, something he insisted was a formidable margin (there have been wider). Boxer stated on CNN that "…in my lifetime, I have seen two elections where the winner of the general election did not win the popular vote." She went on to deride the college as an arcane, undemocratic system that does not reflect the realities of a modern society. She wanted it eliminated for reasons I've stated, but also to assure every American that their vote is counted. To be fair, waxing metaphorically, people were not voting for Trump or Hillary; they were voting for an elector, or electors. They vote for the person who has pledged their allegiance to vote for their chosen candidate. We watch election returns on the night of the second first Tuesday of November, usually knowing the next morning who is going to be the chief executive for the next four years, but the game is not over until the electors vote December 19. In contemporary history, it has become closer to a formality, rarely having any profound effect on what was known in November. The most salient reason for people to oppose the college is that it is not reflective of the popular will of the people. Boxer's legislation never went anywhere.

There exist insurmountable hurdles to the Electoral College's elimination from our government. To abolish it or alter it in any way would require a two-thirds vote in the Senate. It would also have seven years' time for three-fourths of the states to ratify it. It sounds like a laborious process, one that has not been attempted since 1992 when the twenty-seventh amendment made Congress immune to getting big pay raises. The ease of passing an amendment to the Constitution has to do with what is being changed, its popularity and feasibility. The twenty-sixth amendment completed its requirements in a matter of months in the summer of 1971. The eighteen-year-old citizen could vote, but it had at least two decades of history behind it. An amendment to permanently change the face of elections, how a president is elected, requiring some states to cede something from which they for years have perhaps relied on to let themselves be heard, is asking a lot more than merely amending who is allowed to vote in that same system. The proposed twenty-eight amendment would be paradigm-altering, requiring an elimination of a component baked in the Constitution. In a roundabout way, the passage of the twenty-sixth amendment did reform the Electoral College. That is, if 1971's new additions to the VAP, the eighteen to twenty-one-year old's, exercise their hard-fought right to vote religiously in the fullest capacity. They alone can widen the electorate, the grid, the base, and significantly increase the odds of the popular vote determining the electoral vote.

The last time serious intentions of ridding the Constitution of the Electoral College occurred in 1969. Nixon had just defeated Humphrey with a 301 to 191 electoral vote total. However, in the popular vote, Nixon's win was much less, capturing less than half the votes. In 1969, sitting Vice President Hubert Humphrey favored the movement to dump the Electoral College. His impetus to eliminate the college was Alabama governor George Wallace. Running as an American Independent, Wallace and running mate Curtis LeMay managed to scoop up forty-eight electoral votes. The turn of events, the contentiousness of a party that preached separatism after nearly two decades of civil rights legislation, made each major party consider the ramifications of a third-party on the future of politics. Both parties' ears rang with the words of Wallace, "segregation now, segregation tomorrow, and segregation forever." The words brought to the fore the racial animosity America was trying to leave behind. Wallace netted five southern states, the most to date carried by a third-party candidate espousing bigotry. It became a bi-partisan concern, addressed long before 1968. It had to do with the possibility of Wallace winning some electoral votes and possibly causing a tie between Humphrey and Nixon. In such a case—per the Constitution—the president is selected by the House of Representatives, while the vice president is chosen by the Senate. Prior to 1968, randomly targeted proposals to abolish the Electoral College had gone nowhere. Wallace's contentious showing placed momentum behind the idea. Where have you gone Hubert Humphrey, in 2016 this nation cried out for you.

Shortly following his 1968 win, Nixon, as a sitting president, said, "I believe the events of 1968 constitute the clearest proof that priority must be accorded to Electoral College reform." The Republican candidate proposed only reform. Any form of an intermediary system will not constitute direct elections. In April 1969, Humphrey wrote, in an op-ed for the *Los Angeles Times*, "direct election of the president would give each American citizen an equal vote—a fundamental principle of our democratic process." The amendment was the work of the American Bar Association proposing that the president be elected by a popular vote. While Nixon supported this bill, he also crafted his own proposal. He wanted the president to be elected by a plurality of 40 percent of the electoral vote rather than a majority. If no candidate reached 40 percent, a runoff election would occur. Nixon's proposal made it to the House of Representatives where it passed. It did not make it to the Senate until September 1970 where a filibuster was quickly called. Detractors were conservatives from southern and small states, who debated the bill for nine days. A motion was made for a cloture, a process to end a filibuster, which was met with a 54–36 vote. A motion was made to set the proposed amendment aside, opening the Senate to other business. The proposal was forgotten and died when the 91st Congress adjourned. In 1977, Jimmy Carter proposed a number of campaign reforms, which included ending the Electoral College. "I think the amendment process must be reserved for an issue overriding governmental significance. But the method by which we elect our president is such an issue," he said in a March speech. In 1979, the bill introduced by Senator Birch Bayh (D-IN) in 1968 failed to pass the Senate in a 51–48 vote.

In the twenty-first century, manifestation of the drive to move toward a more direct electoral system is known as The National Popular Vote Interstate CompTures ensuring that the candidate who wins the national popular vote will get those states' electoral votes. The proposal passed in eleven states which, together total 165 electoral votes. The chances of the proponents of National Popular Vote getting states totaling the other 105 votes are not great. It is a compromise, one of many solutions, oddly enough (perhaps serendipitously) kind of where the whole conflict of interest began over two hundred years ago.

To the average voter, electors are nameless. They are faceless drones employed to support the candidate to whom they pledged their loyalty. In December of 2004, an elector from Minnesota secured themselves a footnote in history books. They cast their vote, representing 492,000 people who supported vice presidential candidate John Edwards. The elector marked Edwards in both slots, vice presidential and presidential, missing completely the name of presidential candidate John Kerry. The ballot was then seen by a different Minnesota elector who took the Edwards vote to have been made in error. The elector took solace in the fact that the Electoral College wasn't separated by one vote. The rules directed that a tie in the Electoral College be settled by Congress. In the end, in such situations, the decision of a country's president is routinely submitted to a partisan environment, a fundamentally unequal mediator. The college, by design, is at risk of voters going unrepresented, or virtually ignored, by candidates. This is most likely to be the effect in states where one candidate is backed by a strong majority of voters.

By its definition, the role the Electoral College has played in our history, the advantages it's given to southern states in the beginning, the Electoral College system has been a buffer, a "third party," to direct elections. It promises to be around a long time. It may be altered, the sieve, a catalyst between true democratic elections and a decidedly Republican favorability under the pretense of states' rights. When the generation of descendants of slaveholders die out, when time cleanses the political landscape enough for people to know, to dare to appreciate, what a direct election is, then, and only then, can I see the safeguarding Electoral College being wholly expunged from the American record.

III. Raising the Bar

*Democracy is not simply a license to indulge
individual whims and proclivities. It is holding oneself
accountable to some reasonable degree for the
conditions of peace and chaos that impact the lives of
those who inhabit one's beloved extended community.*

—Aberjhani

Some leaders, presidents, banana republic despots, or presidents-elect, don't like numbers. They have an overwhelmingly destructive affinity for themselves, much less for the lackeys with whom they tend to surround themselves. However it's spun, there is much less math to do at the end of it all. Easement with oligarchical trappings, or an outright benevolent dictatorship serving a concentrated segment of America, is much simpler than trying to meet the needs of a heterogeneous country of 327 million. The mid-term election of 2018 was the most dividing in modern times. It also turned out to be one of the most unifying elections. States that had been denied a more liberal sense of ethics became blue at an alarming rate, and rumors of a "blue wave" swelled to heights not seen in decades. After a year of Trump's ignorant, regressive, oppressive, dangerous foreign and domestic trade policy, people saw the unstable wizard behind the curtain. It wore a perverted elephant suit. This was far from de rigueur GOP politics. Static Republicans surrendered their joy buzzers soon after Trump's

2017 inauguration and voted Democrat in the midterm. Many Trump voters suffered from buyer's remorse, perhaps even carrying the stink of doing so until the wash of at least the next two election cycles. Those who did not vote for two evils fidgeted in their chairs at town halls, ostensibly responsible for the embarrassment the world could see, for the thousands of lives ruined and those put in daily fear of deportation, of the continual suffering he caused most Americans as his administration went on virtually unchecked. The confessions were the words of anxiety, of poor judgment, embarrassment, and a soupçon of gullibility. They came from the willing subjects of focus groups. It was tragically surreal as they stared blankly, dissonantly, on cue into a two-way mirror to say the words that long ruminated on the grayest brain matter. The ultimate confession, "I voted for Trump." The words came from educated people who had felt disenfranchised. They came superfluously from the consciences of dissatisfied Americans loathe to admit they had made a colossal mistake.

Enigmatic Trump Voters

I know a family of Republicans who regrettably voted for Trump. I have a whiff of doubt they will again. They are all lawyers, swearing the support to a man who has zero regard for that which they profess to their clients. They are otherwise good, honest, upstanding people. The father of this family once served as a legislator in the Minnesota House of Representatives. The education and law, the values (the son became an eagle scout with me), the claims to Christianity, the incongruence is too much for me.

The essence of shellacking, simply winning big, metaphorically eviscerating an opponent, was around well before Obama. I first heard him use the term in reference to the 2010 midterm loss of the Democrats. They lost sixty seats in the House of Representatives and six in the Senate. The irony is that it was said forty years after the last Democrat won by a landslide (Johnson/Goldwater) by a black man who should best appreciate the opportunity to vote. Johnson signed more legislation to level the playing field for black Americans than any other president, without which a black president in 2008 would never have happened. The integrity, the conviction to a candidate, no matter how they poll, is a learned reaction. Consider 1972, how fiercely people wanted an end to the Vietnam War, how they knew the Democratic consensus was that George McGovern could bring that end. Then I think of people who were delegates for Shirley Chisholm, people who usually supported the candidate with the best chance of securing the nomination. Their brain likely told them that their candidate will not win. The impetuousness youth creates the situation when ideals are placed before reality, to go against the grain, pushing the envelope toward greater good, incrementally closer to that glass ceiling. Logic and numbers dictated that McGovern was the candidate to vote for if one wanted to win in the prolonged balloting that barely kept delegates from sleeping on the floor of the Miami Convention Center at the 1972 Democratic National Convention. For her time, Chisholm did quite well for a black woman, coming in fourth with 152 delegate votes. McGovern, who lost the nomination to Vice President Humphrey four years earlier, easily won with 1,729 delegate votes. Chisholm always said that she faced more adversity as a woman. Her skin color was not the issue. She does, however, stand as the first black female in Congress (1968) and the first black female to be a presidential candidate of a major party (In 1940 Republican Margret Chase Smith had become the first white female in Congress). Almost half a century later, America is close as ever to electing a black female vice president.

Some citizens are more aware than others of their surroundings, the political lay of the land and what is required to keep an even keel. It is both a sense of relief and a low-hung albatross, to know what keys fit a democracy. I was immersed in an atmosphere of political participation. I took it for granted that most people knew that the only way a democracy will function at its optimal level, or even know they do have a chance against the often tricky and deceptive tactics of many iterations of Republican politics. I was, from a formative age, exposed to people who prioritized their civic responsibility, their piece of the pie, the acts that give them a right to bitch about the government if they feel that it does not fairly represent them. Many people, although still not the requirements for a democracy (or even a quorum), probably voted for a president with regularity. I grew up seeing my folks vote no matter how insignificant the election. They voted when all that was on the ballot involved city councils and school boards. Today's members of the city council will likely be running for Congress or president one day. I took note of their proud, habitual, hopeful acts of diligence.

* * *

Often in modern history, it has been idealistic youth that plants the seeds of change. David and Goliath scenarios play out in streets, in schools, in legislative chambers, or even the White House. When gun violence enters the public school system, repeatedly; when the blanket freedom of the second amendment is valued more than the life of a fifteen-year-year old human being; when weapons designed to use on the battlefield are used in the corridors of a high school, it is time to reassess our priorities.

Calls to lower the age of voting to sixteen came because of gun violence. The 2017 massacre in Parkland, Florida, brought about the question. The students at Marjorie Stoneman Douglas high school faced off with Senator Marco Rubio (R-FL), firing at him intelligent, succinct questions to which he could offer sketchy trite answers. They, often at sixteen, won the brief gun debates with the adult politicians in the room. At age sixteen, a citizen can drive, work for the first time with no laws restricting the hours and, therefore, pay taxes. The National Youth Rights Association makes the argument for equality and fairness. Lowering the voting age to sixteen has worked at the local level in two cities in Maryland. To bolster the case for a voting age lower than eighteen, a study in 2006 indicated that there was a "trickle up" phenomenon in this practice. In 1989, state representative Phyllis Kahn (D-MN) proposed lowering the voting age to twelve! In office from 1973 to 2017 in the Minneapolis district now held by Ilan Omar, Kahn was a strong advocate for suffrage of youth populations. In 1991, 1999, 2001, and 2004 she co-authored bills to lower the voting age to sixteen. When young people aged sixteen to seventeen first experience voting, there is often a civic dialogue brought to the table. Parents engage in meaningful conversation about civics with their teenager, a random act that is likely to result in sending them to the polls.

Since WWII, a few members of Congress have coalesced to bring the voting age from its centuries-old twenty-one to eighteen. In 1941, Senator Harley Kilgore (D-WV) first pushed for legislation to lower the voting age. He, along with other senators, representatives, and First Lady Eleanor Roosevelt failed to gain any national support. However, on the state and local level, Georgia passed a bill lowering the age to eighteen in 1943, with Kentucky following in 1955. A year earlier, President Dwight Eisenhower had first addressed the issue of prohibiting suffrage on the basis of age to a national audience. The conscripted service to fight in Vietnam increased the need for a constitutional amendment, bringing the matter to Congressional attention. Pressure grew steadily. Registration and voting participation worked to urge President Johnson to lower the voting age nationally. In June of 1970, President Nixon signed an extension to the Voting Rights Act of 1965, making the legal age to vote eighteen in all local, state and federal elections. He said, "I have directed the Attorney General [John Mitchell] to cooperate fully" as he tested the constitutionality of the lower age. Oregon challenged Nixon's law in court, eventually coming before the US Supreme Court. *Oregon v. Mitchell* debated whether the 1970 extensions to the 1965 Voting Rights Act were constitutional. The decision was split and deeply divided. The court held that the lower age provision was not constitutional as it applied to state and local elections. However, it was constitutional as it applied to federal elections.

When the voting age was lowered to eighteen, the justice of being able to vote on the Congressmen and senators who made laws directly affecting the lives of their younger constituents wasn't enough. Draft-age people went to the polls in larger numbers in the 1972 election, but the youth vote drifted off. The older, professional people, who opposed lowering the voting age to eighteen argued that they lacked the maturity to vote. Granted, the drugged-out hippie wandering the Haight did not make a compelling argument for intellect, but they represented less than a tenth of the boomer generation. By the height of the escalation in Vietnam, the eighteen to twenty-year-old demographic generally knew what was happening in America. They knew why they were being drafted, put in a drum as lottery numbers. They knew the system. They figured it out, if for no other reason than to stay alive. People I know from that era, who were of that age group in the late 1960s, knew the lottery. They knew if their number was high or low and planned their lives accordingly. They made a mature decision they could live with if the chance of being called up was good. They knew their options; dodge the draft and go to Canada, resist and remain in America as an activist, become a conscientious objector, request non-combat duty, get a college deferment, or fight like Uncle Sam wanted.

Abbie Hoffman, Jerry Rubin, many of the Yippie leaders were born before or on the beginning cusp of the boomers. By 1970 most were into their thirties. The Chicago police really feared the influence and leadership of older "intellectuals" like David Dellinger and Tom Hayden. Dellinger and Hayden were leading figures in forming the National Mobilization Committee to End the War in Vietnam, or MOBE. The leaders of these activist groups could vote. Many of their followers could not. Officials in Chicago, police, and city staff intent on maintaining a sense of law and order at the 1968 Democratic National Convention, saw anti-war protest groups like "the Mobe" as being the work of older intellectual activists directing their younger blue-collar followers. Those who "cleaned for Gene" McCarthy in his 1968 campaign for the Democratic nomination consisted primarily of students.

The election of 1968 was one notable example of voting irregularities, fraud, and suppression perpetrated by the Democratic Party. It was, however, within the party and not aimed at disfavoring an opposing party. The Democratic Party had been fractured by the Vietnam war and Johnson's hawkish policies, which seemed more Republican in nature. Robert Kennedy and Gene McCarthy represented a much more progressive and cogent approach to ending the war. The June 5th assassination of Kennedy further split the party with many of his delegate votes going to Vice President Hubert Humphrey, who joined the presidential race soon after Johnson withdrew. Humphrey had suppressed his true intentions to end the war more in the fashion Kenneany or McCarthy espoused. Even with Johnson out of the race, he was still insufferably loyal to him. And so, evolved two camps, McCarthy, and Humphrey. It was a tribalism similar to what has become of the GOP. One could say the party was headed in that direction; Trump closed the deal. And that'd be one successful deal for him.

In Minnesota, three out of its ten Congressional districts went to the McCarthy forces. The southern part of Hennepin County comprised the third, St. Paul the fourth, and Minneapolis the fifth. Minnesota was allotted fifty-two delegate seats with thirteen going to the three districts. In the end, by the national convention, two of the thirteen had abandoned the McCarthy forces for a black caucus led by Cleveland Mayor Carl Stokes. At the convention as well was a McCarthy delegation from Alabama. Much of the black vote had gone to Robert Kennedy, who had been endorsed by prominent blacks like Bill Cosby and those in other minorities like labor leader Cesar Chavez. There was an alternate delegation led by Georgia House of Representatives member Julian Bond. Nominated to be George McGovern's running mate, Bond became the first black man to be a nominee for vice president in a major party. Only twenty-eight at the time, Bond quickly turned it down, citing the obvious constitutional requirements.

Humphrey, having endorsements from the president, Chicago's Mayor Daley, former president Harry Truman, not to mention the "chairman of the board" Frank Sinatra, was nominated on the first ballot. With thirteen delegate votes of the fifty-two combined from the three Minnesota districts for McCarthy, two delegates defected for a black caucus leaving eleven for the senator.

Final Ballot

Major candidates	Delegate votes
Humphrey	1759.25
McCarthy	601
McGovern	146.5

I submit that McCarthy, by the balloting at the convention, where the televised suppressed revolution occurring outside the barbwire that surrounded the amphitheater distracted from the election process, the Minnesota senator did not get, as current Democratic National Committee chairman Tom Perez says, a fair shake. Eugene McCarthy began as a virtual unknown, going door-to-door shaking hands, building a grass-roots coalition of young college students who had cleaned up for Gene. In New Hampshire and Wisconsin that winter of 1968, the tip of the primary election cycle, McCarthy shocked many, including New York senator Robert Kennedy. His initial reluctance to take on an incumbent president subsided after seeing what the young Minnesota senator could do. March was pivotal. In the New Hampshire primary, McCarthy won forty-two percent of the popular vote to the president's forty-nine percent. Four days later, on March 16, Kennedy renounced his prior support of the president's policies in Vietnam and announced his own candidacy. In the April 2 Wisconsin contest, McCarthy raked in fifty-six percent of the vote, outlasting Kennedy, and Johnson with six and thirty-five percent, respectively. Senator McCarthy won the high percentage of votes in PA, MA, FL, OR, NJ, and IL. However, they were just popular votes. On June 4, Kennedy was celebrating a four-point marginal victory (46–42) in the California primary. After declaring "on to Chicago," Kennedy exited the stage of the Ambassador Hotel through the kitchen. There he was gunned down by Sirhan Sirhan, a Palestinian angered by prior politics of Kennedy.

In terms of delegate votes, McCarthy trailed Kennedy and Humphrey who, after President Johnson withdrew from the race, entered in April.

Delegate votes after Robert Kennedy's assassination

Candidate	Delegate vote totals
Humphrey	561
Kennedy	393
McCarthy	258

In 1967 Allard Lowenstein and Curtis Gans had instigated a campaign to "dump Johnson." With the war in Vietnam rapidly and violently losing support, McCarthy as a senator saw the only way to end it was to make it the center of his campaign, a referendum on the ballot. Polls overwhelmingly indicated support for McCarthy and a cogent end to a war, which had at least a year earlier been determined to be futile by its own curators. On March 31, 1968, Lowenstein and Gans succeeded in ousting a sitting president, sans coup, sans bloody revolution. Johnson was the victim of popular vote, primary votes for McCarthy. On a Sunday night, at the end of a Vietnam address to the nation, the president surrendered, saying, "I shall not seek, and I will not accept, the nomination of my party for another term as your president." He surrendered, trusting that his loyal vice president would carry on his hawkish ideas. Apparently dumping a sitting president has no hope of working on a narcissist.

With Johnson gone from contention, Humphrey gained support of labor unions and big-city party boss Richard Daley, Chicago's mayor whose pecker Johnson had long ago pocketed. He benefited from the New Deal coalition, an alignment of interest groups and voting blocs around the country from the time of Franklin Roosevelt. The vice president, who Johnson covertly supported, did not compete in primary races. He had favorite sons, surrogates, to campaign for him. These favorite sons, in addition to endorsing Humphrey, campaigned in their own states for the sole purpose of controlling delegate votes:

- Indiana governor Roger Branigin
- California State Attorney General Thomas Lynch
- Florida Senator George Smathers
- Ohio Senator Stephan Young

After Johnson withdrew from the race, Kennedy acquired many Catholics (a flock fellow Catholic McCarthy hoped to get) and black votes. In a span of two months, black Americans lost their civil rights leader and the presidential candidate many hoped would carry

King's ideas to the White House. Humphrey, with an insurmountable passion to be president, expressed his devastation at Kennedy's death, lamenting, "I don't want to win this way." Nonetheless, the 393 delegate votes won by the late senator trickled down into his coffers. Another voting bloc Humphrey had support from were conservative southern Democrats, or "Dixiecrats." He split them with third-party candidate George Wallace. The Alabama governor, who had said "segregation forever" during Jim crow, now pledged the immediate withdrawal of troops if the war was not winnable within ninety days of his taking office.

Hindsight bothers me, as it did many delegates at the time, that Kennedy virtually hijacked McCarthy's campaign. He was the Sanders of that election. His efforts were essentially eclipsed by Kennedy's prestige and notoriety. As delegate votes went, McCarthy did not get a fair shot, even shake, in the end in Chicago, when keeping youth from exercising their civil rights to protest a war was paramount. The nation was deeply divided by 1968. As body bags returned from Vietnam, as students burned draft cards and effigies of the man who would draft them, the popular vote was McCarthy's, as evident by the count immediately following the primaries that year. After the June 11 Illinois primary, McCarthy had amassed more popular votes than his most notable opponents, especially a sitting president whom he alone may have influenced to withdraw.

Popular primary vote totals

Candidate	Popular vote / %
McCarthy	2,914,933/ 38.73
Kennedy	2,305,148/ 30.63
Johnson	385,590/ 5.10
Humphrey	166,463/ 2.21
Unpledged	161,143/ 2.14

A theory, one that I recently heard a pundit allude to manifesting itself in a way today, limits all the efforts I watched, heard, in our house growing up. It asserts that the more than 10,000 demonstrators who clashed with thousands of police in Chicago may have inadvertently driven less liberal Democrats closer to Republicans. There is a reasonable doubt that fence-sitting doves were turned into hawks. George McGovern affirmed that the protests he observed were not entirely free of violence. There were bad people on "both sides." As with Kent State three years later, the protesters were aggressors as well (they burned down the ROTC building, a strong political statement, but still arson). Some protesters threw stones, even fecal matter, at a Goliath dressed in blue. It is theorized that the Democratic Party may have sabotaged itself by driving law and order voters to Richard Nixon (who was listed as a write-in candidate at the primary level). By vilifying Hubert Humphrey, the once shrill clarion of civil rights who had sold his soul to Johnson in hopes of the presidency, it's suggested that the Democrats may have effectively suppressed turnout of their own party. It is the contention of many academics and *Chicago '68* author David Farber that the rebelliousness during a time when law and order were on the radar sparked decades of Republican rule. I have always thought there was a chance that the whole movement in 1968 might have done more harm than good in the long run. It was what it was, for its time. It was a much-needed vent if only to send a message that at best generated support for the anti-war movement. It sent a message to the people who could stop a war that had been complacently counting casualties since 1965. Minnesota senator Eugene McCarthy put the war on the ballot. The immediate and total withdrawal from Vietnam was a plank in the platform the Democrats brought to Chicago. Two years of work by students, some not even voting age, intellectuals and older professionals for McCarthy came crashing to a halt as tabulation of votes for the plank showed on a monitor on the convention floor. In a vote of 1,567.5–1,041, the war was allowed to continue. I argue that democracy was not an ingredient in the primary race and certainly not the convention.

It is suggested that the Democratic backlash, all the civil disobedience, the venting of frustration of a war that had long ago been determined to be "Unwinnable" (by 1966 Defense Secretary

Robert McNamara had admitted this), played a factor in the alignment of the 1968 general election. One can't argue how history played its hand. It simply stands as a record from which we can learn, one we may learn to regret. In 1948 Harry Truman, after having ascended to the presidency through the death of Franklin Roosevelt, carried on the New Deal liberalism. He ran that year offering a Fair Deal, making civil rights a plank in the Democratic platform as no other candidate had done before (or since). Truman effectively placed the ball in the court of the Democrats, and the American electorate, for the next two decades. The elections of 1952 and 1956 went to a Republican, but Eisenhower was moderate and did little to disturb the trend of liberalism. It is interesting, however, to note that our involvement in what grew into the pointless war that cost billions of dollars and carelessly lost 56,000 American lives began on his watch. Nonetheless, the lies began with civil rights champion John Kennedy and continued with Lyndon Johnson. Soundly shellacking an opponent in 1964 who was said to be as loose a cannon as Trump, Johnson eventually succumbed to the pressure of Vietnam, civil rights, the riots, and the very backlash of liberal protesters. They all worked to morph a man who did more for minorities than any president into someone more politically like the man he beat. In the spring of 1965, determined to make good on the promise of protecting South Vietnam in America's role as proxies, Johnson launched Operation Rolling Thunder. The bombing campaign rained bombs and napalm on the North for three years, each fueling the anti-war movement in America. Marches, protests and demonstrations did play a role in first commencing peace talks in May 1968.

The effort came in phases, waves of anti-war sentiment placed before a hostile witness. From 1964 to 1965, the movement's proponents consisted of many who had opposed the Cold War and foreign intervention, as well as a generation of college students who had lived through the worst Jim Crow South and knew how ignorant the government was to injustice. It began as a well thought out movement, with aims to educate Americans who supported the war with information their government likely wasn't apprised of, a history of Vietnam it did not know itself or did but would not tell the public. When the war proliferated in 1965, the movement took two decisive courses of action; to arm its activists with information about Vietnam sufficient to move others to action, and to make such opposition look less radical, as many Americans felt opposing a war risked their patriotism. In 1966, when draft calls dramatically increased, many middle-class families, with sons for whom military service was not a plan, took note of the anti-war effort. That began a second wave of the movement, peaking the voices of influence such as Senator Robert Kennedy's. In February 1968, Kennedy gave his "Unwinnable war" speech, signaling his clear break with the policies of the Johnson administration. Senator William Fullbright held hearings on the war, bringing the anti-war sentiment to the medium of television. Finally, in May, leaders began peace talks.

But efforts were not all so civil, so organized, so constructive. There were the hippies Allard Lowenstein observed impeding, with intent to derail, troop trains. Blood was dumped on draft records. Political stunts, like the attempt to levitate the pentagon, were carried out by yippie Abbey Hoffman. The band of radicals, known as the "Yippies," entered Pigasus, a 145-pound domestic pig, for president in August 1968. The live political metaphor was a charge (interstate commerce of livestock) cited in the subsequent trial of the "Chicago 8." The civil, left-wing, dovish approach with which the anti-war movement began culminated in the chaos of the 1968 Democratic National Convention. According to some historians, that was the seminal moment, the event, the act of vengeance or disloyalty that realigned the two parties. The election in November codified the ideological paradigm shift. Nixon defeated Humphrey with a modest popular and electoral margin. Nixon's manipulations with a peace at hand (and thus the outcome of the election) notwithstanding, the chaos and violence (on both sides) a civil anti-war effort descended into is said to have pushed fence-sitting voters to Nixon. And so began the Republican reign, the dominant party in the electorate for the next three election cycles, with four years' time off for the good behavior of a humble peanut farmer.

The incidents of Democrats suppressing or manipulating the vote of an opposing party, after Strom Thurmond led a contingent of Dixiecrats from the 1948 Democratic National Convention in protest of Truman's civil right plank, are rare. The outcome of the effort to end the Vietnam War is probably the closest they come. The suppression of McCarthy delegate votes due to both organic factors and those of fate (assassinations) influenced the primary race, the reception at the Democratic National Convention in 1968, and the general election. Peace, unequivocally, was not given a fair chance.

* * *

Ever since civil rights became a narrative in this country, the party that grew away from the South has fought for them. After signing the Civil Rights Act in 1964, Johnson's special assistant Bill Moyers found him contemplative, looking stunned. Moyers asked what was wrong, and his boss replied, "I think we just delivered the south to the Republican Party for a long time to come." The Democratic Party metamorphosized. To understand its transformation, one must first consider that the Grand Old Party, relatively speaking, is not so old. It is younger than the Democratic Party by more than half a century. Thomas Jefferson and James Madison founded the Democratic Party in 1792 as the Democratic-Republican Party. This party opposed the Federalist Party, propelled by notables like America's first treasury secretary and $20 bill insignia Alexander Hamilton. Jefferson's party opposed a centralized government, emphasizing the rights states of a democratic republic need and should have.

In 1828, with Andrew Jackson's manifest transformation of America, a jackass was born. Founded by his supporters, the early incarnation of the Democratic Party favored such things as a limited government, state sovereignty and slavery. They, as today, opposed the big banks. Needs changed in 1854, and with them, priorities. Steam power was peeking at an industrial revolution, lessening the need for manpower, ostensibly that of black men. The nation was divided over many issues, not the least of which was slavery, the morality of it and whether it should be allowed in states in an expanding nation. In 1854, the Republican Party was a northern conception. It came out of a small town in Wisconsin, of all places (home of progressive Robert La Follette and today's battleground), for the purpose of stopping immigration and the spread of slavery. The Republican Party did not exist only in the South. They supported the preservation of slavery. The immigration issue was of much less importance. Seven years later, the conflagration of all those heated debates began, costing 600,000 American lives to preserve not slavery, but the republic for which everyone would ultimately stand. In the period known as Reconstruction that followed the Civil War, the Democrat's disapproval of Republican legislation galvanized the Democratic Party's hold on the South. The party grew to eclipse itself as an ideal political mentality in the South, assuming a position as a defender of a way of life, a rationale vital to commerce. Capitalism was and is the system of which slavery, lynching, Jim Crow, black codes, KKK, every racial and discriminatory practice, is systemic. That way of life was the edification of white supremacy and erection of statues honoring the Confederacy (most of which were molded in the twentieth century as ominous reminders to blacks of who is really in power, a faction of privileged whites that grows smaller each century). World War II loosened that hold, and the decades-old ideologies on the political spectrum began their Great Migration to opposite ends. Until the post-war years, the Democrat's influence on the South was so great that politicians could not get elected unless they were a member of the party. Harry Truman was a southern Democrat from Missouri. He voiced his personal upset at seeing black soldiers, returning from serving their country, finding the same discrimination in the hostile environment they left. He brought civil rights out of the South, setting it on a scale for America to consider with their vote in the 1948 election. Southern Democrats, at their national convention in Philadelphia that summer, threatened a "rump" convention if Truman backed Democrats' attachment of a civil right plank to the party platform. The "Dixie" Democrats proceeded to secede from the party, placing South Carolina governor Strom Thurmond and Mississippi governor Fielding Wright in nomination. Truman stood strong while Thurmond and his insensed band of Dixiecrats exited the convention hall.

The vote was unanimous, and Thurmond and his delegation held the appropriately named rump convention in Birmingham, Alabama, following the Democratic National Convention in the city where democracy had begun over 150 years before. At their rump convention, the hostile Dixiecrats elected Thurmond to run on the state's rights ticket. Truman left a mark in history, defeating Thurmond and Republican Thomas Dewey, by bringing civil rights into the fray, although Thurmond did win over a million popular votes. The South Carolina senator hoped to win enough electoral votes to force a "contingent election," whereby the Dixiecrats could extract concessions from either party, bolstering support for their cause. It was the first time since the Civil War that the South was not wholly Democratic. From 1948 on, the South became incrementally less of a Democratic assurance for a candidate. For the next decade, many southerners still voted Democratic only because they thought of the Republicans as the party of Lincoln and Reconstruction. By signing the Civil Rights Act in 1964, Johnson sent a clear message to those skeleton Democrats that their days were over. Southerners began to defect. Beginning in trickles, they left the party for the Republicans. (And now Republicans are leaving that party.) The South would never return completely. Johnson's act in 1964 was a juncture, and the parties began to re-establish themselves. Continuing the transformation, the polarization of ideologies extended well into the late 60s and early 70s. White southerners were still moving away from the party, while newly enfranchised black southerners voted (and continue to vote) Democratic. I have difficulty wrapping my mind around it, but there are blacks today who vote Republican, even support MAGA. In 1972, in his run for a second term, Richard Nixon unleashed his "Southern strategy" that involved playing to the racism of southern white voters. In the presidential primaries that year, George Wallace ran as a Democrat. Wallace finished third behind Hubert Humphrey and George McGovern with 23.48 percent of the popular vote. It is indeed a disturbing irony that a man who said "segregation now, segregation tomorrow, and segregation forever" in 1968 finished second to a man who had proclaimed "The time has arrived in America for the

Democratic Party to get out of the shadow of states rights and walk forthrightly into the bright sunshine of human rights" two decades earlier. The transformation of the parties, the ideological alignment, was far from complete. Wallace won eight states: FL, NC, MD, MI, TN, AL, SC and TX, splitting MS and LA with Shirley Chisholm, the first black female to be a major party candidate. While campaigning in Maryland, Wallace was paralyzed for life in an assassination attempt. Even if it was not politically motivated as assassin Arthur Bremer claimed, perhaps it was a karmic twist for Wallace, desperately trying to relive arcane ideals, an omen for running as a Democrat.

Ronald Reagan, "the great communicator," codified the South's hold on the Republican Party, strengthening its gravity, echoing its prestige and nobility as the party of Lincoln. Through the latter half of the twentieth century and the beginning of the twenty-first, the South has consistently voted Republican, becoming dependably red. They can be counted on to vote for the candidate who promotes contemporary Republican values such as smaller government, tax policies that hurt the middle and lower classes, and anything that will ensure the continued right to bear arms, no matter how many mass killings occur, and of course the abundantly hypocritical battle cry of pro-life. These are issues, some of which Trump has revealed to be as least as fraudulent as himself. He outed them. The South, some states more than others, are sore losers. Many states seem to have never totally admitted defeat in the Civil War, as evident in the flagrant flying (until recently) of the Confederate flag. In a 2018 runoff election in Mississippi, Republican incumbent senator Cindy Hyde-Smith "joked" with her black opponent, Democrat Mike Espy. The crowd in Tupelo laughed and applauded as she, with a politically leveraged arm over Espy's shoulder, said, "If he invited me to a public hanging, I'd be on the front row." What in god's name would possess anyone to say this? Trump has fueled much of the racism and even white nationalism, a true- blue cousin of white supremacy. Hyde-Smith, an ardent Trump supporter, based much of her campaign on the endorsement of a man who had carried Mississippi by nearly eighteen points in 2016. For thirty years, Mississippi has been steadfastly Republican in who they send to the US Senate. Despite losing to Hyde-Smith in the 2018 runoff election, Espy secured forty-six percent of the vote, the most of any Democrat since 1988 when US Congressman Wayne Dowdy lost to Trent Lott in a 46.1 to 53.9 percent split.

Ever since Donald Trump took office, there has been a steady decline in the redness of the South. By 2018 he was gaining a reputation as the kiss of death for a political candidate. Many southern states did not even want his endorsement. With the notable exception of Mississippi, a state that failed to officially ratify the Thirteenth Amendment until 2013, the South saw Trump's Republican ideas were far from "the party of Lincoln," and calling it such was nothing less than a mockery of Lincoln and a total show of disrespect to its ideals. The GOP has long been wearing blackface, and the Republican voting block is drying up in the South. Lyndon Johnson's lamentation in 1964 that he delivered the South to the Republican Party echoes blissfully, edgily, as Trump's contorted, perverted view of Lincoln, his ironic admiration of Andrew Jackson (who he thought could have stopped the Civil War from happening), unflinchingly hands it back to the Democrats.

* * *

The instances of Republicans being proactive in the field of suppressing votes of an opposing party, in a contemporary context, are numerous. There is a history of suppressing the black vote following the passage of the Fifteenth Amendment. Of course, at that time, it was the southern Democrats slapping hands at the ballot box. It was the Reconstruction South that was resistant to the suffrage rights afforded former slaves after the Civil War. In the days of Jim Crow, with black men being actively obstructed from voting until Lyndon Johnson signed the Voting Rights Act of 1965, a joke among blacks told of a clerk determined to keep a man from voting. It began with the man being asked to read a passage from the Constitution. He obliges. The clerk then asks that it be translated to Spanish, which he does. Other languages follow, all with sufficient renderings. The clerk then asks the man to read a passage in Arabic. He tells the clerk that the translation is "Negros cannot vote in this country." Jokes like this, with little exaggeration in their time, are becoming relevant in today's voting landscape. All that's changed are the methods employed to disadvantage minority voters. Today they have technology to work with, to cloud voting. It is more mechanical and administrative, less practical, and logistical. Literacy tests, poll taxes, and grandfather clauses have given way to somewhat cleverer and less overt tactics. A shining example is the efforts of Georgia's secretary of state Brian Kemp in 2018 to ensure the defeat of Stacy Abrams, former minority leader in the state House of Representatives. Abrams, on election night, was virtually tied with Kemp. Republicans, seeing that they were losing, particularly to a black woman, panicked and cheated. They implemented obscure readings and archaic rules. In this case, Kemp invoked an obscure exact-match law. The law stems from a 2017 Georgia law saying that a voter registration application is complete only if the information on it matches exactly records maintained by either Georgia's Department of Driver Services or those of the Social Security Administration. By doing this, Kemp suspended 53,000 voter registration applications. The criteria for suspension included things as insignificant as a missing hyphen from a surname. The suspension also had a conspicuous disproportion. Blacks comprise thirty-two percent of Georgia's VAP. They accounted for almost seventy percent of the suspended applications.

Kemp begs to be the poster boy for contemporary voter suppression. Bigotry, however well cloistered it is in the shrink-wrapping of hidden voting machines, is palpable. Donald Trump irritated that xenophobic bone in America so easily picked and made oppression of minority groups in the 2018 election that much easier. The issues he raised were fundamental to the future of the American electorate. He once commented that there were too many immigrants coming from "shithole countries" in Africa and the Caribbean. Trump has imperiled the future of voting, but also may have shockingly demonstrated its importance. His claim at a 2018 rally in Montana that Democrats influenced a caravan of immigrants coming from Honduras was damaging. He said they were heading north because they "figure everyone coming is going to vote Democratic." He even claimed that he lost the popular vote in 2016 because non-citizens voted for Clinton. Okay. It couldn't have anything to do with the fact that the GOP had nominated a woefully inexperienced, hostile, divisive, misogynistic, corrupt man who had denigrated every minority group in society?

In his bid to govern the state, Brian Kemp successfully suppressed the minority vote. He then accused Stacy Abrams of encouraging undocumented Georgians to vote. His thinly veiled racism affected the demographic outcome of the election. In 2013, the US Supreme Court decision in *Shelby v. Holder* challenged the constitutionality of two provisions in the Voting Right Act of 1965. It questioned section V of the act that requires federal approval for abridgments to voting laws and regulations by state and local governments. The other discrepancy, which had to do with section IV(b) of the act argued that the methods used to determine the jurisdictions subject to section V should not be based on the past histories of discrimination in voting. In a 5-to-4 vote, section IV(b) was found to be unconstitutional on the grounds that any data used to make such a determination is over forty years old. The court argued the data was antiquated and, therefore, no longer responsive to the current needs of—the electorate? Where's the democracy? Chief Justice John Roberts contended that discrimination still exists, but not enough to justify the "extraordinary" remedial provisions the 1965 act placed on states of the former Confederacy. This is tantamount to saying that the decline in the spread of an infectious disease warrants the halt in vaccinating against it. The analogy is ironic as Trump and his merry band of Republican sycophants wanting to open the economy after only bleak decreases in the COVID-19 case/death rates, and after word was out to "slow the testing down please!" Almost immediately after the court ruling, Texas enacted strict voter ID legislation. Thus began the slippery slope. Soon Mississippi and Alabama issued similar laws. *Shelby v. Holder* augmented the voting restrictions on the six million Americans with past convictions. This meant that in Florida, Tennessee and Kentucky, at least twenty percent of the eligible black population was unable to vote. Repercussions of the 2013 supreme court decision continued to permeate the South, with North Carolina placing sweeping restrictions on early voting.

Evidence shows that not only has the decision made it easier for state and local officials to suppress the vote of black and other ethnic minorities, it also led to the disproportionate disappearance of polls in communities. By 2018, nearly 1,000 polling locations in the US had closed, with many in predominantly black communities. What may seem obvious was researched. A change in voting location, or the reduction of polling places, will have an effect on voter turnout. There were decreases in the allowances of early voting, purges in voter rolls, and enactment of voter I.D. requirements, almost exclusively the work of Republicans. As such, Brian Kemp's strategy in 2018 amounted to "one person, no vote."

* * *

In 1970, Alaska and Hawaii followed Georgia and Kentucky as states that had amended their constitutions to lower the age required to vote to eighteen. The idea of lowering the age to vote was proposed in March the next year, proving to be the fastest passing constitutional amendment in history. The idea of lowering the age of suffrage from twenty-one had more than three decades of activism behind it. It was not a partisan issue. It had endured as the subject of the court cases, and Nixon's trial of the proposal as an extension of an earlier act. The US Constitution was amended for the twenty-sixth time on July 1, 1971, adding 11,000,000 new voters to the VAP. The following year, in the presidential election, there was a new section of voters. The idea was that many of these new voters, the draftees who could pull a trigger but not a voting lever, would vote for the Democratic nominee, George McGovern. They would effectively vote against an illegal and immoral war that had no end in sight. Among many other things on the liberal platform, McGovern pledged "the immediate total withdrawal of all Americans from Southeast Asia." He took a shellacking despite the new cast of voters. The VAP turnout spiked slightly (55.4 percent) that year, but it was not sustainable. Through the next two decades, the propensity to vote declined. The motives were not there. Democracy is not a spectator sport and should not require motivators and cheerleaders to function—even in a limited capacity.

In the 1992 election, the VAP finally buoyed itself, although the voting participation of the eighteen to twenty-four demographic paled in comparison to that of older voters, many of whom saw the younger citizens squandering the opportunity to enact change. Real invested change, proclaimed change, evidently brings out those who can make change. The 2008 election of Barack Obama, the president who broke the color barrier, saw a fifty-one percent VAP turnout. Aside from the cache of being the first black man to find the Democratic nomination, he brought a level of cool pragmatism to the office not seen before. The youth voted for change. They came out to vote because he was the real deal. He was worth the effort (which is perhaps the pettiest thing I've heard) to come out and vote. It seems America can lie on the couch to watch the Olympics every four years, but can't summon the gumption to vote? Since 1972's shellacking of McGovern, those 11,000,000 youth exercised their right to vote with a less implacable and dutiful ambiance than their older countrymen and women. As 1992 and 2008 showed, they were aroused only when the Democratic candidate stood a real chance of winning, usually on the heels of a Republican run of eight or more years that did damage to our democracy. I learned from my first voting upset in 1984 that a good Democrat must be able to lose as well as they can win, to use the loss as a reason to vote with a stronger conviction next time.

Presidential Elections
Voter Turnout for Citizens Ages 18–24 and 25+

Year	Ages 18–24	Ages 25+	Difference Between Age Groups
1972	55.00%	70.00%	16% pts.
1976	48.00%	69.00%	21% pts.
1980	45.00%	69.00%	24% pts.
1984	46.00%	70.00%	24% pts.
1988	42.00%	67.00%	25% pts.
1992	51.00%	72.00%	21% pts.
1996	40.00%	66.00%	27% pts.
2000	42.00%	70.00%	28% pts.
Difference in turnout 1972–2000	-13% pts.	0% pts.	13% pts.

A ten to twenty percent difference in the voting trends of those over twenty-five. The average eighteen-year-old is not overly concerned with politics. Since the Vietnam war, when that age had a much-distempered dog in the fight, the tendency for them to vote has dwindled, with the two noted exceptions. Lower voter turnout trends tend to favor the newest voters. All the work, being victims of police brutality in some cases, going to jail, may have disenfranchised those youths from voting in 1972. When they saw the Vietnam plank in the Democratic platform fail, when Nixon won 43.4 percent of the vote in 1968 to become America's thirty-seventh president, when he immediately began a bombing campaign and set out to expand "the war in ways that Lyndon Johnson didn't dare." They were likely disenfranchised when the Selective Service initiated a lottery to soften the draft, to obfuscate by numbers, capsules, and revolving drums that the government was outright stealing youth to fight their war. McGovern's defeat in a landslide. All were factors to wear away at the effectiveness young voters' perception. Such trends might point to the fact that younger voters will not rush to vote unless there is a good chance it will bring about actual change. That is a rule of democracy; nothing is for sure. You protest, demonstrate, march, and vote at the end of it all and hope for the best. You then work with what you get, plant its seeds, cultivate it into something better yet. The catastrophic presidency of Donald Trump, of a pandemic greatly proportioned by his failure to lead, or even accept responsibility, pushed shove to come. Decades of voter apathy, which, ironically, had a lot to do with Trump's existence in the White House is vanishing as the VAP goes screaming to the polls.

As time went on for boomers coming-of-age, the counter-culture, the anti-war movements, when knowing and communicating about politics was the difference between living or coming home in a body bag, politics became a much-avoided subject. The Trump administration brought the subject much closer to peoples' minds. Democrats were devastated—in many cases to the point of tears— on election night in 2016. Republicans were happy (I guess) that their candidate had won, the tea-party would be heard, and the most unqualified candidate to ever enter the White House would "drain the swamp," build a wall and have Mexico (MAGA donors) pick up the tab. Politics was once again on the table, a concern to only grow as democracy withered. Republicans had it all, three branches overseen by a sociopathic narcissist. Don't forget early January 2017. As president-elect, Trump had plans to get rid of that pesky White House Independent Ethics Committee. It was now a street fight, and generations succeeding the boomers marched, protested Trump, and set up nation-wide indivisible coalitions. They demanded town hall meetings with senators, trapping them in their offices, dying on their lawns, congesting the hallways. Trump made politics necessary again, a needed agent through which Democrats could quell a conspicuously transparent racist who protested way too much ("I'm the least racist person"), who was only in it for the money ("blind trust," emoluments from day one) and whatever the job could do to increase *his* popularity. Trump showed America the power of voting. He showed the devastating consequences of not voting, of voting for a third-party candidate who could not even get ten percent of the popular vote in the primaries. I applaud those who root for the underdog, who theorize that each cycle brings their party closer to serious contention, even if it draws votes from either two-party candidates. But when one of those is so off-the-charts crazy, defying human logic to the point of being a danger, it is not the time to play favorites or root for the underdog. I blame these voters, in part, for the election of Donald Trump. It was the votes cast in states that he won for Jill Stein and Gary Johnson, or those not cast at all, that gave Trump his often repeated and exaggerated electoral win. In Pennsylvania, Michigan and Wisconsin, Clinton lost by a marginal percentage. One could make the claim that if Stein's votes had gone to Clinton, she would have won. I have to question the education, judgment, ethics and sincere desire for America to be either a democracy or a republic that stands for what it preaches, of anyone who thought Trump was more fit to be president than Clinton. Truth be told, few on his staff thought he'd win, much less be presidential timber. With some tugs at stings by Putin, the Electoral College, angry exasperated Republican xenophobes, and an opponent with a history awash in hyped-up conspiracy Trump pulled off a marginal win. He was in the hot seat, much to the delight of the then Republican-held Congress.

On Friday, January 27, 2017, Trump signed an Executive Order banning immigrants from seven densely Muslim countries. The courts struck it down, citing multiple times that its motives violated amendments and civil rights. After over a year of lawsuits filed by Washington state, Hawaii and the ACLU, the Muslim ban 3.0 was upheld by the Supreme Court in June 2018. Trump expressed his undying concern for our nation's security, letting FAA workers and TSA agents go overworked and unpaid in the longest government shutdown in history. The concern for national security was a smokescreen for racism, for xenophobia, for wanting only white people in America. Republicans often ignore the fact, making it easier to fulfill their agenda. In March 2016, the *New York Times* reported that, since 1990, 224 tunnels have been discovered along the Southern border. Drugs come to the US by land—evidently above and underground—by air and by sea. The amounts had quintupled since 2014. The shutdown that stretched from December 2018 into 2019 affected Federal workers, forcing them to go on food stamps in many cases. Trump had made cuts earlier to the budget of the Coast Guard, exacerbating the already compromised branch further by forcing these men and women to work for free (sounds a bit like "involuntary servitude" prohibited by the Thirteenth Amendment) during the shutdown. They were stressed, which means they probably were not working up to optimal effectiveness. TSA agents at airports were calling in sick rather than work for no pay. Air traffic controllers were under more stress than usual. Border control was worn thinner during the shutdown. Does any of this sound like Trump had any real concern for national security? Did he truly intend ever to mitigate his initial assertion that "When Mexico sends its people, they're not sending their best"? And he said this: "They're now sending you. They're now sending you. They're sending people who have lots of problems, and they're bringing those problems with us. They're bringing drugs. They're bringing crime. They're rapists. And some, I assume, are good people." The wall was, from the beginning, something to jog Trump's memory while speaking, a tail to wag at his bidding, a herring, the staple of a red meat diet that was guaranteed to gain the support of the most vehemently racist person on the fence— not "the least racist person." He fed the line, time and again, to a point when a physical structure was no longer the issue, if one had ever been conceived of at all.

* * *

When the pendulous shifts of gerrymandering, voter suppression, the new external manipulations of our elections are factored out of the democratic equation, voting in the 80 to 90th percentile is the critical mass, the democratic exponent. A united front of votes is leverage, an advocate against all the factors which act to prevent any truly democratic system of governance. The concept should be elemental as far as it concerns the efforts to build a more perfect union, to secure the vestiges of liberty for ourselves in the present and future. (oh, that Schoolhouse Rock just wants to play.)

Certainly, every black American has an ancestor who could not vote. Everyone in generation X, or those preceding it, has a mother, grandmother or great-grandmother who could not vote. Many Jews have ancestors who could not vote in certain areas in the eighteenth century. They wanted to vote, to be counted and have a voice in government. They wanted future generations to have this small but critical power in a democracy. So, they fought. They suffered, marched, protested, went to jail and worse. Clearly, the black men and women, the white women, thought that voting would be just as important to future generations as it was to them.

On November 1, 2018, days before a paradigm-changing midterm election, I listened to Oprah Winfrey speak on behalf of Georgia gubernatorial candidate Stacey Abrams. Winfrey spoke passionately of honoring family, of paying homage to legacy. She referenced an uneducated sharecropper in 1946—Otis Moss—who took his reconstructed right to vote very seriously. Directed to another polling place at each stop, Moss had walked a total of eighteen miles by the end of the day, by which time the polls had closed. I had my doubts about the story, whether it was hyperbole or an impassioned metaphor for the human endurance to vote. I've read my history and know all too well the things people did to vote. I also know it is not likely that Oprah would make up a story. I vetted the story to be safe. It happened, and Oprah's reputation remains stellar.

* * *

How come it took over four decades, two generations of idealism, to find that peek again? To vote in massive enough and sustainable enough numbers to dissuade votes in the worst interest of America? In 2008 we saw a surge of Obama voters, young, black, blue-collar voters tired of Bush policies. In 2012 54.9 percent of the VAP voted, down 3.4 percent from the last presidential election. Seems right. Adequate for a democracy, I suppose. Great expectations habitually acquire a slippery slope, at the bottom of which waits voter apathy. People only turn out to vote in peaking values when something of extraordinary contention is on the ballot. An expedient measure of constitutional law, an unconscionable war, an epic event or a terrible president. Any of these will do. They come as things that inspire, and aspire to, a change in leadership. It happened in 2016. Who could have seen a flaw in that logic; that appeasement, the easement, the enraged convenience, the conflation of democracy into some kind of vigilante hijacking in which door number two is offered as a repugnant parting gift, a mantle to be tolerated for four years to the detriment of the majority. There were angry voters, four percent of whom supported the Tea Party. Almost half of them were fair-weather Republicans. They were white, evangelicals, more than half with no post-secondary education. This small band of middle-aged misfits was so disenfranchised they were willing to swallow Kool-Aid left from Jonestown (and later bleach) to make a radical change in American politics. They were dedicated in their intent to "throw a Molotov cocktail" into the system. Guy Fawkes would be proud. A small conglomerate of Americans had their collective craven hearts set on imploding the government from within, of introducing a human element so foul and ill-manned, so unconventional and foreign to any semblance of political protocol, that the system would be changed by the mere process of assimilation. Donald Trump did not coin the term swamp. It had been bubbling away, with a newt leading the descending House, for years complacently submerging reptilian remains from the staff of Nixon and Reagan. The ecosystem Trump promised to drain became a catalyst for the worst politicians ever born, appointed by someone who lacked an ounce of political experience.

The event that happened on October 7, 2016, was the "surprise" for which quadrennial Octobers are known. It galvanized the theory already held by many that Trump's minions were impervious to obscenity, controversy and overt immorality. It reinforced the notion that Evangelicals are sanctimonious phonies who are motivated by anything but god. The vulgar assertions made by Trump were, however, entirely fitting with his character as the last chronic misogynist to walk the earth. He claimed he could "do anything," even "grab them by" well, you know. He said they, I'm guessing this is the media, will let him (or even Billy Bush) do this because of their star status. Well, after October, things went south quickly, and when government is involved, I must concede, that is not normal. Technical things in transitioning to a "president" were overlooked, beginning and ending with ethics. In April of 2017, Trump, in defiance of all predecessors, refused to divest himself of his business holdings, quite consciously, undoubtedly intentionally, leaving himself a clear path for business capital from those holdings to reach him during his stay in the White House. He was evasive in turning over his tax history, a formality to which all presidents, even Nixon, have adhered. He said, on more than one occasion, that they were being "audited." Well, that alone sends up a red flag. Something is anomalous on the records to warrant an audit.

An alternative fact claims that roughly forty family members and their connections benefited from the presidency of Ulysses S. Grant. Eighty-four years later, after JFK chose his brother as his attorney general, a law was passed prohibiting nepotism and exploitation of the power of the office of President of the United States. Trump ignored it, implicitly and complicitly, disrespecting any facet of an office that has been sufficiently and duly respected forty-four times before. His daughter, Ivanka, was marketing her wares made in Asian sweatshops on the White House website. Family connections: Kelley Anne Conway endorsed Ivanka's product on FOX TV. Donald Jr. and Eric profited in the blind trust by using the president's power and location of his hotels. Foreign dignitaries seeking Trump's favor stayed at his hotels in Washington and around the world. His children run the family business and take ski trips at our expense. Taxpayers send Eric and Don on safari to shoot endangered bear. My question is, why this does not seem to bother the Republican voter while the government allotting a minimal sum of money for a SNAP program is a cause to read the riot act.

If any political ne'er-do-well can motivate people to vote against them, Trump is the king, the Forrest Gump of presidents. Everything he did leading to the 2018 midterm election was more immoral, mean-spirited, and more unconstitutional than the last. To repeal natural citizenship, drawing critique from his own Speaker of the House, takes a lot of nerve, desperation and fear. In the early days of voting, in mid-October, people of any age, gender, color, creed, sexual orientation descended like locusts, frogs and boils upon the Pharaoh Trump. Women, of any color, won big. Millennials proved to be the most politically active generation, the most motivated youth movement since the baby boomers.

Descendants embracing fossils of their heritage finally have an active voice in government. Sharice Davids and Deb Haaland were the first Native Americans elected to the US Congress. Ruth Buffalo was elected to the North Dakota legislature, another first for the state. She won in spite of North Dakota's ID law. In a Sioux nation, where Native Americans were suppressed, Standing Rock, the 2018 midterms garnered a voter turnout that was up 105 percent from 2014. Buffalo unseated Randy Bohening, the State Representative who was the primary sponsor of the ID law designed to disenfranchise Native Americans.

History repeats. It plays back again. . .and again, riding a wave of mediocrity to the cusp of insanity. Republicans saw they were losing. They saw that for some reason, Trump's message of fear, hate and divisiveness was not resonating well. It was, after a year and a half, turning people off, dissuading them from voting for any legislator who would support, even inadvertently, such vitriol. His endorsement had come to be the Judas kiss. Following a visit by Trump, a candidate's poll numbers dropped. So, they cheated. Voter suppression was an issue in red, carnivorous North Dakota, where thousands of Native Americans reside where the streets have no name. Their addresses as registered voters were PO boxes. In Georgia, Stacey Abrams was running to be the first black female governor of the state. Her challenger, incumbent Brian Kemp, hid massive amounts of voter registrations. VAP turnout was so high, unprecedented numbers won Democrats back control in the House of Representatives despite all the tricks Republicans offered to suppress them. An estimated forty-seven percent of the VAP voted in the 2018 midterm election, up from just 36.7 percent in 2014. These are midterm elections, after all. They provide a chance to regroup, to make an educated assessment of the president. I see it as an opportunity to amend what the executor—or in this case circumventor—of law, must work with for the next two to four years. The House of Representatives and the Senate make the bills the president signs into law. My theory is that McConnell and Ryan only put up with the juvenile petulance of Trump because he was willing to sign pretty much anything put in front of him by a Republican-controlled Congress. The craven malevolent hearts and minds of these legislators waited their entire careers for an executive like Trump, inexperienced, gullible, void of any distinguishable character, integrity or moral compass.

Less than half the VAP voted, beating the odds, thwarting the cheating GOP strategies. Imagine what would have happened if 100 percent turned out in a midterm election. Unlike the presidential election, there is no Electoral College in the midterm, no buffer between the majority in a democracy and the one percent who buy and sell America at will. In the midterm, one person one vote is a reality, although the Senate is not proportionate to the voters in a state. America is not quite a true democracy, but in the midterm election, it is as close as it comes. That is, if everyone participates, if everyone black or Native American votes unimpeded, there will be a fair representation

of what America wants. That never happens: elections' fate is baked in the cake. Weeks after the 2018 midterms, even with just over half the VAP participating, the message was loud; THEY DO NOT WANT TRUMP!! It was loud enough in 2016 from 55.7 percent of the VAP, but the popular vote does not ultimately decide presidential elections, an elucidation that may itself trump the concept of one man, one vote.

The Electoral College stands like a giant authority, a second voice, a lever to pull, an oval to fill, that ostensibly makes ours on the ballot void. It is a scam in a true democracy and does its best to discourage voter participation. In a presidential year, the first Tuesday after November 1 is a formality. December 19 is when the real decision is made, when the Electoral College casts its votes for whomever they pledged their vote. There are a total of 538 electors in the college system, 270 of whom a presidential candidate needs to win. A state is allowed the number of electors equal to that of its Congressional delegation, plus two for each senator. Minnesota, for instance, has ten electoral votes: that's one for each of the eight Congressional districts, plus one for each of its senators, Tina Smith and Amy Klobuchar.

December 5, 1804, arrived after a month-long election. Incumbent Thomas Jefferson (Democratic-Republican) defeated Charles Pinckney (Federalist). The Twelfth Amendment to the Constitution had instated upon the new nation the system by which its presidents and vice presidents were elected. That first election utilizing the new method of buffering the votes was a landslide. Jefferson won 72.8 percent of the popular vote and ninety-two percent, or 162 of the available 176 electoral votes. Did founding fathers rig the system, or was it rigged over time, with the rigging untangling itself to comport with the trappings of history? An Electoral College acts as a brilliant filter of voice, a muffler, a homogenization process of the American people, an assurance that the product was (until 2008) white as milk. It acts as a plot twist intended to keep the populace from having a direct one-on-one contact with a president. As we see today (most recently 6/1/20), that one percent, that billionaires' boys' club, is terrified of the WE that struggles to intubate We the People. The Electoral College was a safeguard, a security system. A state's electoral votes are determined by the number of Congressional districts it has, which is determined by population. Electoral districts used to be the products of legitimate malapportionment. They had a divergent ratio of eligible voters to representatives. Consider two Congressional districts, one has 20,000 voters and another has 200,000 voters. People comprising the 20,000 voters have twenty times the persuasion, per person, over a governing body. Even that, the legit fit, might be rigged. It may implore a favorable outcome for one group in a swath of voters. It may even be deliberate, favoring the equality of groups rather than the equality of individuals. The proportioning and equal representation of states in legislative chambers has been mitigated in the US Supreme Court. In the 1964 court case *Reynolds v. Sims* a ruling stated that electoral districts must be "roughly equal" in population. The case was brought by M. O. Sims, a voter in the state of Alabama. Several states had failed to reapportion their district voting lines recognizing the changes after the 1940 census. Due to the High Court's ruling, it was found that voter to representative ratios as high as 1081:1 existed in legislatures. The inequality in representation might be appreciated another way. Consider the smallest percentage of voters that could plausibly win a majority of the governing body. It likely would be due to the gross disparities of the populations of the districts that voted. Suppose that a governing body had eighty-one members. This is half of the voters in the forty-one districts with the smallest populations. When fewer than fifty percent of the VAP wins a majority of the governing body, it is influential. It is a codifying moment in electoral outcomes. But is the outcome realistic, plausible enough to bank on happening again?

In modern history, when there have been prolonged bouts of political apathy, peaking during midterm elections, more or less than half of a voting-age population participates in a democracy. How could that ever completely succeed as such? That's why we can only, as former President Obama said, "aspire to the better." A perfect democracy in America has never existed. It will not exist in anyone's children's lifetimes. I predict one of three scenarios happening: 1) the democrats will do what they can to save humanity, make life fair for everyone and the GOP will resurrect itself like a broken cross and continue the fight to be America's alpha dog; 2) a third party becomes a viable contender in elections picking up at least twenty-five percent of the vote; 3) some president in the future, having Trump as precedent, will succeed in his nationalism and America is under new management, sure to go the way of the Roman Empire. I chose to stay cautiously optimistic in the age of Trump, always knowing the grim realities possible. It went my way. I won as a Democrat, sadly something I have said with sparse comparison to graciously, hopefully accepting defeat. The media conveyed a kind of unspoken, subdued optimism leading to the 2018 midterms. Democrats had learned a lesson with the cocksure attitude of the 2016 presidential election when they were the hare and Republicans the tortoise. They won back, with an affable margin, a majority in the House of Representatives. Over 113 million Americans cast ballots in the 2018 midterm election, easily the highest turnout for such an election in US history. It was the most virulent show of democracy since the Vietnam war protests. From November 9, 2017, to November 6, 2018, the principles basic to a democracy were rigorously exercised with a tenacious regularity. The first women's march was attended by 500,000 (roughly the number that comprised the "Woodstock Nation") gentle souls who opposed Trump's zealous deportation policies and unconstitutional rhetoric. That size increased exponentially as the divisiveness and economic consequences of his trade wars were anticipated across the nation and in the world. Between 500,000 and 1,000,000 in Washington DC, up to 5,600,000 nationwide, 5,000,000 in the world. Protests erupted in Europe as they sensed the worst foreign policies coming out of the United States likely since LBJ. Every state in the union held rallies in one or more cities, plus the territories of Puerto Rico and Guam. That's participation, a majority showing their disapproval of a man his second day on the job. We could do better. We could hope for better. When Trump first tried to execute his Muslim ban, thousands of protesters and pro-bono attorneys flocked to Sea-Tec International airport. In the end, the courts ruled the ban unconstitutional, largely because such little thought had gone into the Executive Order. It is in our favor that Trump is inexperienced, prone to failure, incurious, impulsive and outright lazy. And then there was the "March for our lives," the largest of the gun violence protest organized by survivors of the Parkland, Florida, school shooting. In Washington DC, over 700,000 young Americans participated in democracy on March 24, 2018. Surely all of them (eighteen and older) voted, having vowed repeatedly to vote out senators who accepted money from the NRA or voted against proposed gun legislation.

The situation for Democrats looked better after the 2018 midterm—a lot better. It was a tally in the House that kept getting better and better as states such as FL, GA, AZ and CA were in contention, demanded recounts by Trump or the Republican candidate, or just were historically slow to count votes. The expected duration of the Trump Administration got worse. With control of the House, Democrats had free reign and were able to investigate Trump with more invasive rigor. They could, for instance, subpoena his complete tax returns. These would surely reveal with whom Trump was in bed. His financial holdings would become fare for the media. And, we could finally know why Trump has a lip lock on Putin's backside. It did get better for the Democrats after the 2018 midterm, but things were not perfect, which is par for the course of democracy.

It was on New Year's Eve 2018 that I first heard that Senator Elizabeth Warren (D-MA) was officially running for president in 2020. She is a champion of the middle-class, often sharing her personal stories of feeling the weighing down by the upper-class. I was not surprised then when she unveiled her "wealth tax" in early 2019. Warren's plan taxed the ultra-wealthy, which comprises nearly 750,000 households in America. It consisted of a 2 percent tax on households with net assets over $50 million; 3 percent on assets $1 billion. The super-rich have been parasitically living in the laps of luxury off the middle-class for decades, even centuries. Most Republican administrations end up levying a tax in spite of what they promise, and the middle-class takes another hit. Trump's tax cut was the extreme circumstance. It was destined to make the super-rich—himself included—richer, and the middle and lower-classes bore the brunt. Every chance they get the super-rich tilt the playing field a little more to favor themselves. Warren's plan intended to reverse this. It would, in simple terms, recoup over years the millions that have gone to the lifestyles of the rich, the big bank CEOs, the pharmaceutical companies, the infinite salaries of Congressmen. The money would be in the GDP to invest in programs that could create opportunities for ordinary people to have an equal shot at pursuing their own happiness and financial security. Warren's idea was not without precedence. Taxing the mega-wealthy has been tried in other countries, notably Switzerland, a country seventh on the list of full democracies. Warren was counting on her tax to put $2.75 trillion (over ten years) back into the economy. As in Switzerland, and other developed nations, the prospect loomed that the target group would find ways to avoid paying it. There are always those in any group who find loopholes in the tax system, however, people like Trump evidently have made it ubiquitous to the lifestyles of the rich and famous.

Taxing the super-rich has been on the decline. Its enforceability is always going to be variable in its success. A 2016 study by the National Bureau of Economic Research found that for every 0.1 percent of taxation on the wealthy in an area, the assets the wealthy reported to the government dropped 3.5 percent. In a democracy economic equality, even the white male has a dog in that fight, is resistant to change. No one has really addressed the glaring anomaly in America's fundamental financial structure like Warren or Bernie Sanders. Those who voted for Trump, stood by him while he made America the laughingstock and patsy of the world, those working-class people go to work each day, year after year netting around 45 to 50K annually, and sense nothing wrong with that. There is no disparity. They are complacent, perhaps support the NRA with their membership, and don't want for a better life, more opportunities for themselves, their children, or anyone else in the world. They watch in apathy as the likes of Trump, or Reagan before him, introduce programs that give the right-wing advantages that rarely trickle down to them on a lower hanging branch in the conservative hierarchy. It is natural selection. It's the origin of the species. Religion (if not science) has taught them that. They don't buy into evolution, so it follows that some construct of how the economy could have evolved in a more equitable fashion is just as incredulous; bang… one percent of the people will keep amassing more money than a human can spend in ten lifetimes, and nothing should be done about it.

* * *

Many impediments exist for the eighteen to twenty-nine-year-old voter. A logistical problem faces them at once. The act of voting— and registering to do so—is a first for many. Some are so confused from what news they follow that they are surprised when they are not asked for ID at the polls. Youth are sometimes transient, often not maintaining the same address for more than a year or two. They forget to update their residence or register to vote after they move. To the average eighteen-year-old, voting likely came in last, if at all, of things to do for a move. Hopefully, as the tenure of Trump has revealed the ugliest consequence of democratic ignorance, that mentality will change. Eligible voters under twenty-four have the poorest turnout of any demographic. It may have a lot to do with recent hurdles legislators have set before college students. In July 2018, Governor Chris Sununu (R-NH) signed a bill requiring students to provide proof of more than a residence in a dormitory to vote. It ended with a judge ruling that the state couldn't make new rulings during a midterm election. However, what was tried in New Hampshire had success in other states in the South. For decades in Greenville County, South Carolina, it was the practice to have voters who listed Furman University as their address fill out an extra form when they registered to vote. It asked if they owned a car, were employed, and if their parents still claimed them as dependents. It was intrusive, extracting needless information that could be used against them. In 2016, three students sued the county and had the form banned. Another deterrent from youth voting is that the laws are constantly in a state of flux. When one is trying to earn a degree, better their life, work a job or two, they may not have a lot of time to keep themselves apprised of the voting procedures. Some Republican legislators understand this and seizing upon it and exploiting it to lessen the vote count in a group more statistically prone to vote Democrat.

In 2010, Republican state legislatures set about closing polling locations and reducing voting hours. They also passed new voter ID laws making it difficult to register and vote. Florida Secretary of State Ken Detzner was accused of a "voter purge" (begun by his predecessor, Kurt Browning). In 2014, he attempted to ban early voting on college campuses. That ban was eventually overturned in a US district court. It adds up and poses the suspicion that Republican legislators are chomping at the bit to find more ways to extract youth from the voting equation. On average, young people and college students will vote Democrat, something counter-productive to any Republican agenda. The nation's largest historically black college is North Carolina A&T. In 2016 the student body, which comprises 10,000, was divided in half by Republican legislators. The school was redistricted. The college, which had operated under African American alumni, fell into the district of two white male Republicans in 2016. Tactics to discourage youth voting in New Hampshire, which had a rich history of blocking student voting, included making the owners of cars re-register the vehicle with the state in order to register to vote. The law fundamentally was the poll tax of Reconstruction times by requiring excessive car registration fees and was rendered unconstitutional.

If the climate's ripe enough, tipping the scales unnecessarily to the right, youth voting prevails in the end. Between the 2012 and 2016 elections, despite all the impediments, voting among college students increased by more than three percent. There is a psychology driving it all, making it work, warding away apathy. There is often an idealism in youth, a daunting apparition of the world that festers in projection. A feeling of control, no matter how minuscule, must register. Young voters may feel that their vote will not matter, or make a difference, and they may ask themselves, "why should I bother to vote?" As such, issues are a constant to the young voter. What is important to them, or what they deem a responsible issue for society as a whole, they change. In recent history, it became gun control in the context of the Parkland, Florida, school shootings. If it did not wake up lawmakers, it did wake up the youth of America to the fact that they were being gunned down while in pursuit of an education in the pursuit of happiness. It woke them to challenge a heinous insanity that has been allowed to go on in America. The issue comes down to bartering young lives for the prosper of the NRA, special interests and the careers of spineless, unconscionable politicians suffering from chronic greed. Following the Parkland 2017 Valentine's Day massacre, students at Marjorie Stoneman Douglas High School rose and took on the NRA, succeeded in getting sponsors to drop them, and wounded the giant. They met with senators and plainly stated their demands, even extracting a few noted words of conciliation from Trump. But perhaps the most valuable accomplishment, one that has lasting power, was to enlist a whole new crop of young voters, many of whom were of voting age in time for the 2018 midterm. Their actions resulted in eleven states passing legislation that will keep guns out of the hands of people linked to domestic violence. A federal ban on bump stocks was passed, and Florida raised the age to buy a gun to twenty-one.

In 2018 Democrats took control of the House of Representatives, not the Senate. Sometimes voices are stronger than votes. The Senate votes on laws that are open to the quips of special interests but are also influenced by a Democratic House. Senators might have had their conscience on guns raised by the Parkland students. In the end, the power of opinion often exceeds that of a vote, the rallying call and personal tales of gun violence by those too young to vote. Gun control is among other issues brought to the fore in 2018; the reproductive rights of women is now a concern of millennials. The addition of Niel Gortech and Bret Kavanaugh to the Supreme Court made the reversal of laws, including *Roe v. Wade*, a realistic possibility. Climate change was also invigored by Trump's pulling the US out of the 2017 Paris Climate Change agreement. Younger voters are enraged about police brutality (and further agitated in 2020). The Trump Administration was the common denominator. His toxicity and total ignorance of any sense of Democracy, and the office of president, woke what is a formidable force in voting.

IV. The Suppressed Vote

A political science professor once began a lecture on why people don't vote. Why will their vote count in the end. He began with the analogy of cheering on your preferred sports team. A simple comparison, but with the Electoral College, that is about the size of it. Factor in voter irregularities, fraud and active voter suppression—foreign or domestic. The popular vote is indicative of the people, obviously, in a democracy. It reflects who the majority want to win, just as in a football game the team with the most fanfare is usually favored—or at least wanted—to win. Any American who knows anything about our political system knows that the Electoral College is the deciding factor in a presidential election. As a Gen-X Luddite, I sometimes like to savor how relatively impervious to foreign intervention our elections were in the days before the internet. I like to remember the days before tweets, a social media when Moscow troll farms could not breed a maligned candidate like Mrs. Clinton. In times of great contention, recounts, voter irregularities (Bush/Gore in Florida, 2000 and Franken/Coleman in Minnesota, 2008), ballots were hand-counted. The time would be swapped essentially. Pandora is out. There is no total recall. But it is nice to think about the option, the better ghosts of elections past. If America had invested half the time it has trying to get Trump out of office in hand-counting ballots, keeping the whole Democratic campaign offline, Clinton probably would have turned out a marginal electoral victory, having avoided the shrewish, scornful image social media gave her. We would exchange the hardship of hand-counting ballots for the inevitability of foreign interference, of a hostile power "grooming" a candidate, Manchurian or otherwise, who is likely beholden to them. You can't go home again. It is the information age, and the question who needs this information, why, and how will it be used, is asked far too seldom.

From the beginning of America, as a sovereign nation to the end of the Civil War, the white males over twenty-one were unchallenged. Blacks could not vote, women could not vote, young students or young men under twenty-one could not vote. The voting coterie had their treehouse and the ladder to gain entrance was not there for over a century. There was no reason to suppress anyone's vote. In 1870 the Fifteenth Amendment to the Constitution gave African American men the right to vote. They were US citizens, as established in 1868's Fourteenth Amendment. As such, their right to vote ". . .shall not be denied or abridged by the United States or by any state on account of race, color, or previous condition of servitude." The delicate balance of the republic was upset. Men who had for years counted as three-fifths of a man for electoral purposes were now a whole entity, able to physically, cognitively vote themselves. During the years of Reconstruction, Southern Democrats felt threatened as never before and suppressed the vote.

Was voting important to the treehouse exclusions simply because they couldn't, because some entity of entitled men was making all the rules and they had no say? For many decades anyway, after the prize was won, the right to vote was not taken for granted. The slogan "old enough to fight, old enough to vote" was heard in the '60s as young men were sent against their will to an immoral, illegal human atrocity on the other side of the world. No one suffered physically so an eighteen-year-old could vote, but demonstrations and protests went on to raise consciousness in the years and months before 1971.

Politically interested Americans have been conditioned to watch for that magic 270 electoral votes on election night. They know, deep down, that the popular vote, which was their two cents, does not win elections. In this way, until less importance (or none at all) is placed on the college, America will only be a democracy in theory—kind of like "all men are created equal," "We the people," or "of, by, and for the people." That is a gut punch, a bamboozle. It is a heavy distraction from voting, a reason to throw in the towel and not be heard at all, to remain silent in the bleachers as your team loses (or wins). You can't claim any credit, real or perceived. In the 2018 midterms, many races were close, within 5,000 votes or less. One could realistically suggest the scenario of a razor-thin margin in which one vote could conceivably turn an election. Between eight o'clock and nine o'clock pm central time on November 12, Krysten Sinema was declared the "apparent" winner of the Arizona Senate race. Sinema claimed the seat of the mealy-mouthed, aptly named, retiring Jeff Flake. Her Republican challenger Martha McSally delivered her fireside concession speech. Their race was never more than two or three percentage points apart in the final months of the race. The final tally came to 48.0 percent for McSally to Sinema's 49.7. In another California House race, over a week post-election, Democrat Katie Porter led Mimi Walters by an ultra-thin margin. In elections like that, in midterms where the vote is the vote and nothing's farmed out to a higher power, some archaic conglomeration in which the voter is at best a weak-toothed cog, the voter realizes the importance of their vote. They can really be a player in the game. The Democrats kept winning, something at which I remember hearing the Trump Administration would excel to the point of boredom. Jared Golden defeated incumbent Bruce Poliquin to serve Maine's second Congressional district. The potential victories, an unwavering propensity to flip House (and the odd Senate) seat, proving a vote matters, lasted weeks after the election. The 116th session of the US Congress began in January 2019. It was a house divided, with Republicans holding the Senate and the Democrats the House. They picked up thirty-eight seats in the 2018 midterm, the biggest yield since 1974.

The majority spoke—over 113 million. After a year and a half of Trump's reckless global posturing, his careless regard for anything that does not have anything to do with him, and his repeated reluctance to flatly denounce the far right, an increased (from 2017) percentage of America abandoned him. They leaped screaming from the Trump train as they saw him fixing his time machine for 1920. Never was democracy threatened like it was by Trump. From his "zero tolerance" policy that resulted in the virtual abduction of children from parents, and their being detained in cages, to his dogma that climate change is a hoax invented by the Chinese, Trump gave America every reason imaginable to push for someone better.

* * *

America is changing. Attitudes, motivators, and quite literally, the fatal consequences of not voting are shaping the voter and, thus, the electorate. I ask you to compare voting consistently to paying your taxes every year on time. Although that act is emboldened by the omnipotence of the IRS and the proven reality that not paying them will eventually land you in jail. There is no coercion to vote. No one will audit you or give you an orange jumpsuit. On the contrary, there was a time when people were faced with jail if they attempted to vote. In these cases, they did vote, or try, and suffered the consequences. It meant that much to them. The suffragettes who protested in 1917 went to jail for under a year. As a point of protest, they twice chose a significantly long and brutal ("Night of Terror") incarceration rather than pay a fine of $25 ($553 in 2020 spending power). To many, there is no incentive to vote or not to vote. Some people are indifferent to the concept. When that indifference is left alone to consume itself as other pressures and opportunities of young lives reveal themselves, it is a short walk to apathy.

The economy, the war in the Middle East, the promised change in direction, may have had something to do with voter turnout. In 2008 younger voters went to the polls in greater numbers than was seen for many years. Every fifth or sixth election cycle, every misconceived war a successor has planted, every steady economy that is torn asunder, a politician comes along who is compelling enough to bring dormant voters out of their corners. Roughly forty-nine percent, the second highest in history, of people eighteen to twenty-four years of age turned out to vote for Barack Obama. Expected to be high, the total number of voters was 131.3 million. That was an increase of roughly 9,000,000 from the 2004 presidential election. The architects of a fallacious war, Bush and Cheney had worn out their welcome, rode their wave of popularity for waging (and carpetbagging) a "war on terrorism," pushing the boundaries for torture after the 9/11 attacks. Democrats flocked to vote for John Kerry to replace a president they thought had, among other things, opened a Pandora's box in the Middle East, employing a "back door" draft to fight his war. It was one of the first times a concerted effort to "get out the vote" took hold. In October that year, I attended a "vote for change" concert featuring acts like Bruce Springsteen, Neil Young and John Fogerty. Entwined in the music were messages of how Bush had squandered our economy and started an unconstitutional, frivolous war. Baby boomers to generation X and beyond were implored to go out and vote, to effectively "fire a man" who had violated or ignored the constraints of his job. The total voter turnout was 56.7 percent of the VAP. Four years later, after the economic larceny of Bush, the momentum that drove youth to the polls was still there, with more force.

2008 Presidential Election

Candidate/ running mate	Party	Electoral vote	Popular vote / %
Barack Obama/ Joe Biden	Democratic	365	69,498,516/ 52.9
John McCain/ Sarah Palin	Republican	173	59,948,323/ 45.7

VAP turnout had risen to 58.2 percent! It was the highest rate since 1968, the year Johnson was sending young men overseas with many coming back in body bags. Getting rid of a bogus, criminal, scandalous or incompetent president in their first term, ending a war, or just a radical need for change during the nation seem to be what motivates people to vote. The idea of a black president was long overdue, and a young well-spoken, pragmatic, freshman senator resonated with voters. To make the effort to vote, one must be sufficiently upset and significantly frustrated to make that paltry effort (in most situations) every two years. I may be biased because never in my life have I had to wait more than twenty minutes to vote at a polling place that was conveniently located. Even so, I know how crucial an ingredient voting is to a democracy, one that will not be said to have derivative flaws "baked in the cake."

For at least the last two generations, voting has been taken for granted. In the 40s, 50s and 60s people voted, the people who, for example, fought the noble wars. Military Service and voting participation are relative. Older people, all eligible to vote, fought the first and second world wars. Kennedy was drafting from a younger demographic when it came time to send troops to Vietnam. Until 1971, when Nixon further complicated a war already boiling over in opposition, many draftees and enlisted men could not vote. The older demographic votes today. Their parents voted. The younger generations, my generation and beyond for a long time did not vote. In the twenty-first century, certainly the 2016 election and the 2018 mid-term, the VAP turnout is high for obvious reasons. The best thing to come out of a Trump Administration may be how it sent at least two/thirds of Americans to the polls en masse, perhaps making the power of voting as elucidating as ever. It's signaled a wake-up call, an alarming reality that is too often eclipsed by alternate "realities." America was at once reminded of the sleeping giant, grown complacent, spoon-fed pablum from the start that it is #1, the greatest nation in the world, all that rhetoric (fading fast) about being the "land of opportunity." America, the implicit democracy, is none of that without 100 percent VAP turnout. No one has, since 2016, said America is #1. Trump has lost the respect and trust of its most ardent allies. He burned the NATO bridge, and if America ever found itself in a war, none of those allies would be contractually obligated to help. And given America's track record for prolonged wars, fighting futilely, I doubt they would volunteer.

I suspect that to many, the prospect of a President Trump was daunting, if not outright terrifying. To many, though, Hillary Clinton was equally as bad for America. It was all the baggage she carried; the stigma of Bill, the Benghazi grilling parties, the unfounded accusations the right-wing media had drilled into its legions of FOXhounds' brains. And then there was the voting contingency who wisely decided not to vote, or better yet, chose this election to throw their vote to a third-party candidate. And there, by the grace of the Electoral College, Trump went. By the grace of the college and his puppet-master working strings high above Red Square who'd been grooming the incorrigible real-estate failure since the early 80s, he got some free real estate on Pennsylvania Avenue. Who shows up at the polls has a lot to do with the current events, how upset or, in this case, forgotten people feel. A lot has to do with the candidates as well. What scandals have plagued them or their relatives, how gullible one side is, how educated they are, how much they are willing to let someone invent their reality.

Trump won 304 Electoral College votes. The thirty states he carried included key and swing states like IA, AZ, OH, PA, MI and FL. FLORIDA, FLORIDA, FLORIDA. He won Florida by a narrow margin, under 200,000 votes. The more diversities, the greater number of interests a state represents, the greater its swing. The sunshine state has, in modern history, been the least "safe" state. It can't be relied on to vote for either party; it does not paint itself into a red or blue corner. It acts as a catalyst, reflecting the pulse of the nation while also directing it. Each election it eliminates America's vile, pent up, quadrennial waste, a dripping sieve from the peninsula it is. Votes go there to die or be counted once or twice. Rarely in history has a candidate from either party won the White House without winning Florida.

Florida's Voting Record in Presidential Elections

Year	Candidates	Percentage split	Winner won FL/party	VAP % of FL
1916	Wilson/Hughes	69.34/18.10	Yes/D	
1920	Harding/Cox	30.79/62.13	No/R	
1924	Coolidge/Davis	28.6/56.88	No/R	
1928	Hoover/Smith	56.83/40.12	Yes/R	
1932	FDR/Hoover	74.49/24.98	Yes/D	

1936	FDR/Landon	76.08/23.90	Yes/D	
1940	FDR/Willkie	73.99/25.98	Yes/D	
1944	FDR/Dewey	70.32/29.68	Yes/D	
1948	Truman/Dewey/ Thurmond	48.82/33.63/ .15.54	Yes/D	
1952	Eisenhower/ Stevenson	54.99/44.97	Yes/R	
1956	Eisenhower/ Stevenson	57.27/42.73	Yes/R	
1960	Nixon/JFK	48.49/51.51	No/R	
1964	LBJ/Goldwater	51.15/48.85	Yes/D	74
1968	Nixon/Humphrey/ Wallace	40.53/30.93/ 28.53	Yes/R	79
1972	Nixon/McGovern	71.9/27.8	Yes/R	72
1976	Carter/Ford	51.93/46.64	Yes/D	77
1980	Reagan/Carter/ Anderson	55.52/38.50/ 5.14	Yes/R	77
1984	Reagan/Mondale	63.32/34.66	Yes/R	75
1988	Bush/Dukakis	60.87/38.51	Yes/R	73
1992	Clinton /Bush/ Perot	39.00/40.89/ 19.28	No/D	83
1996	Clinton/Dole/Perot	48.02/42.32/ 9.12	Yes/D	67
2000	Bush/Gore	48.85/48.84	Yes/R	70
2004	Bush/Kerry	52.10/47.09	Yes/R	74
2008	Obama/McCain	50.91/48.22	Yes/D	75
2012	Obama/Romney	50.01/49.13	Yes/D	72
2016	Trump/Clinton	49.02/47.82	Yes/R	75

Florida's demographics are constantly changing. The ethnicities of counties change, and the state goes against the consensus of the country very rarely. Richard Nixon won Florida in 1960 as John Kennedy carried twenty-two states having the sum electoral votes—269—to win the White House.

1960 US Presidential Election

Candidate/ running mate	Party	Electoral vote	Popular vote/	States carried
John Kennedy/ Lyndon Johnson	Democratic	303	34,220,984	22
Richard Nixon/ Henry Cabot Lodge Jr.	Republican	219	34,108,157	26

With Alaska and Hawaii having acquired statehood the previous year, it was the first presidential election to have the participation of fifty states. It also marked the last time the losing candidate won Ohio, a swing/battleground state that has also proved its vote to be a metric of electability. The election had its spurious variables, such as voter fraud and faithless electors. Allegations of Kennedy benefiting from the ties his running mate Lyndon Johnson had to Illinois power boss Richard Daley surfaced. They claimed Kennedy fraudulently won that state, as well as Johnson's own Texas, fifty-one electoral votes that would have given Nixon one vote more than the 269 needed to win. Electors in some southern states were faithless, refusing to cast their vote for Nixon or Kennedy, and voted for Virginia conservative Senator Harry Byrd. In the states of Oklahoma, Mississippi, and Alabama, a total of fifteen electors bolstered Kennedy's overall electoral count. His victories were marginal in at least twelve states to the point of contention, and the Nixon campaign advised recounts in some, including Florida. A winning presidential candidate would not do so without Florida for another thirty-two years.

The 2016 presidential election was not a popularity contest. Still, Trump ran as a populist, and surprised everyone, including his campaign staff and maybe himself, with how many people responded to the glib, divisive message he stumped for almost two years. On Tuesday, November 8, 55.7 percent of the VAP came out to vote. The least acceptable consequences of not voting, or voting for a distant third party, were severely underestimated. The frustration factor was in the Republican's favor, having manifested itself in the Tea Party. Obviously, the thought of Donald Trump, a seventy-year-old man who mocked a disabled reporter, who spoke of grabbing women by the short hairs, sitting in the Oval Office was not upsetting enough to make Democrats put aside their apathy or personal beefs with the two-party system and go out and vote. The Tea Parties, the hostile Republican remnant spin-off, need to be heard, their need to throw a figurative bomb into the system, regardless of its less appealing characteristics, was just that strong. Consider this as a metric for how warped, how morally deficient, a small percentage of America has grown in five decades. Consider their level of tolerance for corruption, obscenity, and the overt unrestrained violation and blatant desecration of democracy.

Lyndon Johnson rose to the presidency through assassination, left with a war that assumed that communism had to be contained. He was left to curate a war with the limiting intentions of his predecessor. He was also charged with advancing the civil rights dialogue Truman opened. On the latter score, he won the approval of many Americans as indicated by his landslide victory in 1964. His Civil Rights Acts and Great Society program, his Medicare program, changed America irrevocably. They gave it legs to stand on in courts for decades, and bootstraps when a nation needed them the most. Then, after his good works were appreciated, as they were struggling to be put into practice, someone a little better than a Trumpish figure emerged. The obscenities are there, perhaps more vulgar than Trump. The skepticism I have of the worst LBJ stories I have heard are born out of the simple fact that they are so incongruent with the way he is seen in newsreels in a presidential capacity. I just cannot see a man resting his phalanx on the desk in conference during his job. I have no trouble, though, believing the bathroom consults. That is crude, unprofessional, but efficient. The bravado, the bragging of getting more women than JFK, the notion that a bird in the dark is worth at least two in the bush, is no stretch. Still, America once almost unanimously voted for this man. Had he remained in the 1968 race, I can't say with absolute certainty that he would not have won a second term. In the areas of vulgarity, infidelity, and paranoia, he rivaled Trump. The difference is Trump is always publicly and professionally obscene (which makes me wonder what he's like privately), and exhibits his complete lack of presidential demeanor on camera, all the time, as well as on the multitude of tweets his opposable thumbs produce. I shudder to think what Johnson's tweets would say. We have tapes as a record of how abrasive, profane and racist Nixon was. In 1968, he nabbed 60.7 percent of the popular vote, managing to overshadow the other 40 percent with rhetoric that he would provide law and order on our streets (Trump put a new spin on that). He also vowed to end the war with honor, a promise that was fulfilled as much as Trump built a wall and had Mexico pay for it. He did make it possible, created a situation, for POWs and troops to come home. I'll give him that. But he did not end the war. He essentially left an unstable situation, a civil war that America and allies, following the French, bogged down in for thirteen years.

Nixon's first term also yielded the Twenty-sixth Amendment to the Constitution. By July of 1972, young men who had been old enough to be drafted into a war were able to have a say in that coercion, where it came from, and the characters of the people making the policies that determined their fate. The novelty of the amended age would soon wear off and revert to a historically low number for the demographic. Fifty-five percent of voters age eighteen to twenty-four did go to the polls that year, creating a record. By 2000 that number had dropped to 42 percent. It was symptomatic of the fact that in the years prior to and following 1972, young people were not exactly encouraged to vote, given feedback that made them feel as though they had a stake in the game. Some states require people to present ID to vote. It cannot be assumed that an eighteen-year-old will have a driver's license, voter ID or passport. Unless the young men are being forced to go around the world to fight a war, or young women face serious threats to their reproductive rights, a fighting sense of apathy can't be far off.

In 2018, when the Republicans were trying to hold their control of government at any cost, when Donald Trump was reaching ever deeper into his worn bag of hate, a familiar kind of voter suppression surfaced from the swamp. It lacked the imagination of the suppression that was the momentum of the 1965 Voting Rights Act. Bigoted Republicans hid registration applications, changed the polling place or voting rules, or simply hid voting machines. Over five decades have passed since

Bloody Sunday, and someone in the backrooms of the GOP came up with new ways to suppress the black and Native American vote. America is like a story of a quorum of lost, disfranchised, potentially evil white men who found some land, cheated its inhabitants out of it and established their own rules about who could come in and participate. They made very sure that no one who could upset the order of things could have a vote. Over decades, this changed. The order changed. Compromises were made, and the ever-growing majority spoke. Laws were written, amendments to the Constitution passed. In the twenty-first century, in a midterm election when the majority can change who makes the rules, when the majority can vote out those descendants and disciples of the original white men, the Republicans are down to a few stale fighting words.

Participation in democracy is its own demise. At the onset of what was symptomatic of a gradual failure to significantly be representative of a majority, the criteria to vote were many. The original participants in democracy, in the experiment, were likely to own slaves. At the Constitutional Convention in 1787, it was proposed that slaves be counted as three-fifths of a person. This was figured into the total for a state when appropriating the allotted number of representatives, and therefore electors. So white men who had land, owned slaves, were an asset to their state. In the thirteen colonies, young men could not vote. Very few people were voting from the start. They faced fines or went to jail for trying to vote. Apathy, or the argument that a vote will not count, was not the issue in the early days of voting. In 1787, in thirteen states, the chance of one vote mattering in an election was good. If people said things like "your vote counts" back then, it was not hyperbole. (It still sometimes is not). It was literal, whereas today, it has a smattering of truth in a far less tangible sense. It might be more truthfully put that "your concern counts." It is important that individuals are involved in the workings and the stewardship of their government.

The election of 1824 was notable as the first of five times when the winner, John Quincy Adams, lost the popular vote. Prior to the election, the Democratic-Republican Party had won six consecutive elections opposing the Federalist Party, which was emulative of today's Republican Party. Four years earlier, James Monroe had virtually swept the colonies of the popular and electoral vote. A tiny contingent—0.5 percent or one of the 231 votes available—of a district in Massachusetts voted for John Quincy Adams, who ran as an Independent Republican. A razor-thin margin slices votes cast by privileged, older, white men. A small divide of the party that today has been allowed to gain control of all three branches of government. In 1828, from Friday, October 31 to Tuesday, December 2, Andrew Jackson, who, in 1830, signed the Indian Removal Act, was given a second chance to run against John Quincy Adams. He won with John C. Calhoun, who was equally as pro-slavery, at his side.

1828 Presidential Election

Candidate/running mate	Party	Electoral vote	Popular vote/ %
Andrew Jackson/ John Calhoun	Democratic	178	642,553/ 56.0
John Quincy Adams/ Richard Rush	National Republican	83	500,897/ 43.6

It wasn't a landslide. No one would get "shellacked" for at least another 150 years. The resin was not invented until the twentieth century, and the term as it is applied to a candidate who is washed out was far from being in the ever-changing political lexicon. Jackson won fifteen of the twenty-four states in the union. In 1828, a little over half the voting-age population turned out to vote. A slight surge in voter turnout could have much to do with the fact that suffrage was extended to non-property-owning white men. The total US population was around eleven million. Less than half of that number could vote. Voter participation was paramount when only a limited number of people could. Turnout at the polls spiked during wars, contentious issues, or when the country approached a major crossroads. . .like today. In 1876, an election in which the winner did not win the popular vote, Rutherford B. Hayes faced off against Samuel J, Tilden. The country was at a crossroads. Peoples' votes decided how to move forward after a period of Reconstruction. That year the turnout of the voting-age population, or VAP, (which now legally included blacks) was 81.8 percent. Thousands of émigrés came to this country from Europe in the mid-nineteenth century. Most eventually became citizens and, as such, had a vote in our democracy. According to records found by the Minnesota Historical Society, gaining US citizenship in the nineteenth century was relatively easy. The immigrant had to show up at his local "court of record." This was a random court that kept permanent records of its proceedings, verdicts, of its comings and goings. There, before a judge, they declared their "Bona fide intention" to become a citizen of the United States of America, to renounce allegiance to their former country (in 1967 the Supreme Court struck down most laws banning dual citizenship), signing documents attesting to this as the judge watched. The votes of industrious young men were wanted. They were encouraged so they would bolster the VAP. Few permanent records of women exist prior to 1920. They could not purchase land or homestead, but most of all, they could not vote.

During the period (1890–1910) following Reconstruction, turnout of the VAP dropped, reaching a low of 58.8 in the election of 1912. Historians consider it to be a critical juncture in politics. Democrat Woodrow Wilson was challenged by Progressive Party candidate Teddy Roosevelt, Republican William Taft and Socialist Eugene Debs. However, in those twenty years, Southern states had disenfranchised many African Americans and poor white voters. Then women won the right to vote. In 1920 the turnout of the VAP was 49.2 percent but had risen to 61.6 percent over the next thirty-two years. WWII and the Korean War contributed to this surge in VAP turnout. During the years of the Vietnam War, when having a voice at the table seemed to matter most to people, the parents whose son's fate was really in the hands of the government, and by the 1972 election when the sons had a voice, the VAP turnout was still never significantly more than half. At the beginning of America's involvement in the war, it was in the 60 percent range, bound to steadily decline. By 1996 voter apathy had set in; people had grown complacent during Clinton's first term. That year only 49.0 percent of eligible voters turned up to vote. Subsequent

VAP turnouts rose a few points, barely passing 55 percent in 2016. In that year, it became more and more clear that America was losing, or had lost, any trace of a democracy. How could anyone have known what the result of not voting for a much more tempered, qualified, thick-skinned candidate would be? Who knew Trump came with puppet strings attached that were wrapped around Putin's finger, that he would so easily sell out America to the Russians, the Saudis, and the fat little rocket man with the Moe Howard haircut?

* * *

Senator George McGovern (D-SD) did not even carry his home state in 1972. John Hospers and Theodora "Tonie" Nathan were on the ballot in Colorado and Washington for the recently formed Libertarian Party. People vote their conscience, most often, even if it is against the odds. Hospers and Nathan scored 3,674 votes, not even enough to win a state. The party did gain a following (on the 2016 ballot), and it marked the first time a Jewish woman won an electoral vote.

1972 Presidential Election

Candidate/ running mate	Party	Electoral vote	States carried	Popular vote/ %
Richard Nixon/ Spiro Agnew	Republican	520	49	47,168,710/ 60.7
George McGovern/ Sgt. Shriver	Democratic	17	1+DC	29,173,222/ 37.5
John Hospers, Tonie Nathan	Libertarian	1	1	3,674/ 2.8

Votes count toward milestones. Their calculated sum totals can, over many cycles, begin to wash out an individual's held values, what they really want as a return on their investment. In 2016, people had choices other than Trump or Clinton, a pairing of evils which apparently often ended up canceling the other out. Voters could give their vote to Jill Stein (Green Party) or Gary Johnson (Libertarian Party). I personally know people who did. It was a stand, symbolic, rebellion. The law of averages suggests that a third-party candidate is incapable of winning a presidential election in America. The closest was in 1912 when Teddy Roosevelt ran as a progressive for a third term. I encourage it, voting out of the mainstream. If no one did, many possibly good ideas would never make it into any stream of consciousness in a nation securing the right to free speech. I will say, however, that the 2016 election was probably not the one to wade against the current. I could see that Trump was a loose cannon the minute he stepped on the debate stage. He was a charlatan, bereft of any moral fiber and totally unfit to be president. He was the kind of person who would fight to take away that freedom of speech, the very freedom that gives third parties a voice at all.

CNN polling suggests that voting for third party candidates was in Trump's favor. Had the votes in the nip-and-tuck pools of Wisconsin (10), Pennsylvania (20), Michigan (16) and Florida (29) gone to the Democrats, Clinton would have defeated Trump by earning 307 electoral votes. So, it is argued, a topic for debate of disgruntled Americans whose hopes for a better tomorrow, for at least four years, have been dashed. The act of filling in SAT-like ovals at the polls has either been emboldened to repeat itself, or the bank of apathy has been fed. When a third party has done well enough to contend, to swim in the mainstream, its protractors are drawn out of their vacuums. The feeling is that their chance is now. Who knows when it will come again? Bush and Gore stimulated the mainstream, nothing too dangerous, nothing threatening the very democracy on which it all was based. Bush was a Republican and preached a smaller government. He raised taxes to favor the wealthy, let jobs go, started a war that was, in principle, like Vietnam, a war he sat out in an inactive national guard. In Iraq, we were the proxies who by 2006 had lost their way and questioned who we were really fighting. He knew what he was doing, though. Unlike Trump, W did not violate his Oath of Office less than twenty-four hours after taking it.

For years, Ralph Nadar has refuted the accusation that he drew votes away from Gore in 2000. The late (2008) Tim Russert always told us that Florida was the state to watch. Nadar and LaDuke had won popular votes in Florida and New Hampshire as a third party. At the time, the Green Party was nationally recognized. Nadar and LaDuke appeared on ballots in forty-three states and DC. The Reform party was a contender in the 2000 race. Pat Buchanan, the nominee, began to gain support from white nationalists, getting him an endorsement from David Duke.

2000 Presidential Election

Candidate/ running mate	Party	Electoral vote	States carried	Popular vote/ %
George W. Bush/ Dick Cheney	Republican	271	30	50,456,002/ 47.9
Al Gore/ Joe Lieberman	Democratic	266	20+DC	50,999,897/ 48.4
Ralph Nadar/ Winona LaDuke	Green	–	–	119,000/ 2.74

In October of 1999, real estate mogul Donald Trump joined the Reform Party at the urging of Minnesota Governor Jesse Ventura. Trump had quit the Republican Party due to conflicts of interest (political expedience). He did file to appear on the CA primary ballot, winning 37 percent of the Reform votes cast. Trump soon after withdrew from the race, quipping "The Reform Party is a total mess! You have Buchanan, a right-winger, and you have Fulani, a Communist, and they have merged. . .I don't know what you have!" The 2000 presidential election ended in the Supreme Court. With 51.2 of the VAP turning out, votes being recounted, votes suppressed, there was plenty of room for error. Third-party candidates do help an election but draw votes away from the favored candidate. They provide an alternative for potential voters who don't like either of the two parties' candidates.

In 2016 Libertarian candidate Gary Johnson and Green Party candidate Jill Stein were on the ballot in the general election. There was Evan McMullin of the Independent Party and Darrell Castle of the Constitution Party. They were decoys in this race, lightning rods for Trump. Everyone who voted for one of these candidates didn't vote for Clinton, the favored winner. Few, if any, favored Trump. *The Arizona Republic*, a newspaper that hadn't endorsed a Democrat for decades, endorsed Clinton. *USA Today*, not known for endorsing presidential candidates, printed an anti-endorsement disclosure that declared Trump "unfit for the presidency." *The Atlantic*, a journal in circulation since 1857, endorsed Clinton. She was its third-ever endorsement following Abraham Lincoln and LBJ.

With all that controversy, all that media disapproval, Trump was still able to muster 46.1 percent of the popular vote. Gary Johnson received 0.99 percent of the popular vote, the most of any Libertarian in a presidential election. Together Johnson and Stein gathered roughly 1.3 percent of the popular vote, enough to turn the tide of an election, of any wave that has been gathering momentum. In the 2018 midterm election, votes were counted in a Senate race. They were recounted up to four times, always ending in a tie. A single ballot was found in an envelope, misplaced, not included in the hand recounts. Such occurrences are rare but had happened twice in that election year. Rarely do recounts affect the outcome. But it happens, could happen, and give the benefit of the doubt towards a fair and equal democracy. I contend that the results from 2016 were far from fair. The playing field was heavily to the advantage of the "Republicans," having little interest of containing a democracy. Over-confident Democrats had crunched 538, flushing out all possible paths to 270. And as election day approached, each candidate having pocketed their states in the primaries, the road to the White House for each candidate became more apparent. By the end of October, Trump had virtually no chance of victory. In Michael Wolff's book *Fire and Fury: Inside the Trump White House*, he writes that Kellyanne Conway—the steadfast lackey to Trump and darling of FOX news—the afternoon of November 8 prepared herself for ignominious defeat. She was sure he would lose and probably would have secretly bet against him. Conway did, however, contend that he would quite probably hold his defeat to a six-point margin. Everyone on the campaign, save for Steve Bannon—who insisted his low poll numbers would break—knew Trump would lose. They all had an unspoken thought: Trump will lose, and he probably should not have even run for president—a little white truth that has plagued the minds of most Americans.

* * *

A quorum is of a point of law. It is not even technically required to have a democracy. It is a concept, a benchmark, of parliamentary procedure, the business model in which all orderly social interaction functions. It is in the language of governmental debate. Historically it refers to the number of justices of the peace required to be present in an English court. Although it has been a guide for years, a minimum requirement of people to be present at a deliberative assembly to conduct business. Transactions could be conducted with fewer present, but it would not be legal, official, valid, or kosher.

The number constituting a quorum is set in the deliberative body's charter, by-laws, or standing order. The restraints of holding a quorum to proceed with business, the outcome of which may well affect a nation, can be contentious, even malicious. On February 25, 1988, Senate Majority Leader Robert Byrd tried to call the House to order after the minority Republicans walked out of the chamber. In anticipation was a marathon session over campaign finance reform in the Congressional election, Senate aides had brought cots into the Senate cloakroom. The Republicans had attempted to deny the Senate its quorum. In the end, Byrd's motion to call the House to order was approved in a 45-3 vote. Forty-six arrests of Republicans were made.

It is human nature to find a way out, to sabotage the very system or institution to which they contribute. For better or worse, history has proven that it is in human nature, at any level, to intentionally prevent a necessary requirement for a systemic outcome. Humans are natural-born "quorum busters." In a deliberative setting, a proposition whose end result may be beneficial to the group as a whole, and individual will deliberately try to "bust" that which may have the end result of bringing people together, creating a more equitable living environment, for just maybe bringing—god help us—peace on earth.

A school of psychology agrees that most human animals will eventually discover that they have a need to belong to something, that there is a void in their work-a-day lives. Whether that need is filled by committing to attending or joining a church, the Boy Scouts, the NRA, 4-H, the Young Republicans Club or the DFL (Democratic-

Farmer-Labor), there are rules and charters based on infinitely tedious by-laws. How badly do people want or need to belong? Is it realistic to expect them to attend all the meetings? No. No one does, which is why in an assemblage such as the DFL, which is full of intricate and binding mandates, alternates are chosen for each delegate past the caucus level. In the not-to-distant past, in elections where the fate of a democracy was not on the table, participation in the first step of the nominating process (the precinct caucus) was rarely anywhere near many eligible voters. In 2008, for instance, the median caucus participation rate for Republicans was 11.1 percent, a trend since 1984. In 2004, however, George W. Bush ran unopposed in the primary for his party's nomination, and fewer "patriotic" Republicans participated in the electoral system.c

Evidently, it is unrealistic to expect people, at any level, to be wholly representative of themselves. There is a tendency toward apathy the more secure factors like a candidate's chances of winning become. This was the case with the unopposed George W. Bush. Individuals, the greatest future presidents even, will risk life and limb to "bust" a quorum. They sometimes intentionally upset the predetermined number required to advance an agenda. It's the ugliness of politics, the counter-productivity. When Lincoln was in the Illinois legislature, finding that the doors were locked to prevent such evasion, he jumped out of the first-story window in a failed attempt to bust a quorum. A story like that has got to be true. But even if it goes in the bevy of honest Abe lore as an inspirational exaggeration, the common voter, the constituent, the man or woman who's not necessarily political, whether they like it or not, do have a vested interest in democracy, even if they do not always participate. They bust a quorum of proportions most can't or won't fathom. To them, it seems abysmal because the aims to assemble quorums have many times been the victim in history, repressed and suffocated beyond a common human expectation. Quorums have been the victim of gerrymandering and the Electoral College, shattered beyond all human relevance by voter suppression and intimidation. In the 2018 mid-term election, repulsed by Trump, many still feeling the sting of buyer's remorse, the lingering stench for which they held their nose, voters went to the polls in record numbers. They surfed high on the "blue wave," euphoric with a vindictive spirit of beating Trump at his own game. LGB and TQA all gained positions at either the state or federal level. Diversity flourished, and democracy could gain its breadcrumbed ground. It slipped through that window Abe opened as the cruelest Conservative administration to ever set up shop on Pennsylvania Avenue busted the fundamental concepts of America, its laws, and constitutional amendments.

The 2018 election did have the highest voter turnout (49 percent of VAP) in a mid-term election since 1914 (37 percent). Midway into Woodrow Wilson's first term, a wave occurred. A surge in voting in mid-term elections does not ensure such a turnout of the VAP in the general election. The chances that the "blue wave" will be caught again, or that the surfers never stopped riding it, in 2020, are rather good. Tales of voter suppression, of foreign intervention, of the trolls of social media, are already surfacing. "Let's start playing offense a little bit." Senior political advisor and senior counsel to Trump's reelection campaign Justin Clark was heard extolling their campaign's great concern for voter suppression. He conceded that, historically, it has mostly been his party suppressing votes, after which he vowed to protect our (Republican) voters. Clark reiterated Trump's commitment to preventing voter fraud, a statement that is void of any plausibility, much less credibility, after his acquittal in the Senate, his obvious indifference to corruption, and his firing of an ambassador—Marie Yavanovitch—committed to fighting it.

A Trump-ish candidate, a ringer, a stench-bearing populist is like a divining rod as president, a strip that attracts opposing votes like flies. It did not hurt that in 2018 many states held "special" hotly contested elections. The political contentiousness was palpable, and quorums were easily met. Is that what it takes to move voters, to get them out? Evidently only in opposition to the most repugnant, malfeasant, rapacious, inexperienced candidate, do voters come out to vote. But there have been terrible presidents before. However, I will say the 45th has shown no shame in his propensity to undercut democracy, to express his love for the most ruthless dictators in the world. Who before him has taken it that far, has gone that far out of his way to overtly obscure, pervert, and outright nullify American ideals? Who before him has been such a buffoon on a world stage, snubbing our allies, and selling our loyalties to the highest bidder? James Buchanan, Andrew Johnson, Richard Nixon, any president who has done reprehensible, corrupt things not always in the interest of the country, at the very least had some fundamental understanding of the job.

Obama saved America from the economic meltdown eight years of Bush caused. He killed the mastermind of 9/11. He signed into law legislation that improved the lives of millions. But most of all, Obama showed us what America could be when *everyone* had a stake in the game. As the first black president, without scandal, he was I consider the anti-Trump, the antithesis in every respect. Just his willingness to hand the keys to Trump, to brief him, as is transitional tradition, is emblematic of his class and professionalism. He left withered in his wake much for Trump to resent, from the decades-long birther jabs to just having an incident-free eight years. The fact that a black man who was not a celebrity and had not grown up having money given to him at will, rose to the presidency might have upset him also. A polarizing effect took place in 2016. Even though the most experienced nominee ever lost by almost three million more popular votes than her opponent in yet another electoral defeat, Trump has rarely missed an opportunity to purport its small margin to be huge. Everything is in perceptions' proportion; his, from the crowd at his inauguration to a phallic member he brought to the Republican debate stage.

The suppression of voting has a rich history in America, and that is one of the contributory factors that keep democracy to be a work in progress. Few times in this country's evolution has an entire representation been allowed to vote. Until 1920, there were brief occasions in which women could vote. Almost a century of a democracy functioned with more than half of the US population not voting. After the Fifteenth Amendment, southern democrats devised literacy tests and box rules, peppered with intimidation, the keep the black man from voting. It is always a religion, ethnicity, gender, or race. It may be a person's national origin that precludes their vote. All are subject to be held against an individual in their attempt to vote. Amendments need to be written with the small type, disclaimers that "the government reserves the right to revoke these provisions at any time." Until 2017, because of democracy, the constitutionality of such a sudden revocation could be argued in court and appealed up to a judicious Supreme Court. The voter suppression occurring in the era of Trump is not so amenable.

V. Importance of a Midterm

If you don't vote, you lose the right to complain.

–George Carlin

The functionality of the three branches of government should be co-equal and dependent upon the other. Legislative works with the executive, because of it, never for it. The judicial works independently, for the most part, of the other two. Its justices are appointed by the president and subject to the approval of the two Houses of Congress. They each have their respective functions as outlined in the Constitution, and they have been followed with some relatively inconsequential distortions until 2017. Since the legal declaration of war on Germany, Italy and Japan in 1941, the observance by either party of the war powers act has been negotiable. It has become entirely acceptable for a president to declare war, commit ground troops, without the approval or even knowledge of Congress.

As the name suggests, the midterm election occurs in the middle of a president's four-year term. One will be held for, if there is a god, Joe Biden in 2022. They are an opportunity for a party to lose or gain control of the Senate or the House of Representatives. Seats are added or subtracted to give them a majority or minority in either house of Congress, to the 100 seats in the Senate or 435 in the House. In November of 2020, the Senate seat of majority leader Mitch McConnell is up for re-election. Democratic Iraq war veteran Amy McGrath is running against him to fill the Kentucky seat. In South Carolina, Jamie

Harrison is running against spine donor poster boy Lindsey Graham. Harrison, if victorious, would be the first black US Senator from that state. The Twenty-second Amendment limits a president to two consecutive terms. There is no such limit on the tenure of a legislator. If they can keep getting elected, the job, its salary, benefits, and prestige are theirs. This is evidently a cultish, all-consuming, mind-numbing, prospect. It leads serial senators down that path of degradation; each term robbing them of any integrity disabling their moral compass. During the Trump administration, there were a handful of senators that stuck out as particularly spineless and continually voted in line with a corrupt president. Lindsey Graham, Mitch McConnell, and Susan Collins needed to go. Collins of Maine (running against Sara Gideon), along with Lisa Murkowski of Alaska and Mitt Romney of Utah, were among a shortlist of Republicans whose X-rays showed traces of a spine. It was, more than once, hoped they might cast an opposing vote defeating many Trump policies that were cruel, unusual (Eight Amendment violations), and far from democratic. Collins was a letdown, every time, from the Kavanaugh hearings to the Senate impeachment trial in December 2019. Oddsmakers in Vegas could get rich betting on the votes of these Republicans. Mitt Romney, however, defied the odds by voting to convict Trump at his Senate impeachment trial, two decades after the impeachment began for a president his offenses dwarfed.

If a president is awful, terrible for the country and the world, a category most will agree Trump falls into, the midterm provides a chance in that four years for Americans to assess the job. But it also is an opportunity for voters to use the legislative branch to mitigate some of the damage a terrible president can do. After 2016, Democrats were virtually powerless to stop the Trump administration from essentially destroying a functioning democracy. The federal circuit courts were the sole means of mitigation, of intervention, and litigation. It began with a victory that defeated the administration's poorly executed Muslim ban. Numerous environmental regulations the Trump administration attempt to repeal were invalidated by federal courts. In October 2017, California sued the US government, its Bureau of Land Management, for obstructing a law aimed at preventing waste. Judge Catherine Blake held that the Administrative Procedures Act was being violated.

During his first summer in office, with the courts being the last line of defense against a reactionary extremist, Trump expressed his intent to ban transgender individuals from military service. In usual trite, pedestrian, suggestively hyperbolic fashion, he did so on twitter. As was the method of his madness for most mandates, this was a reversal of an Obama administration decision. Four out of five courts found the ban unconstitutional, and it was appealed to the supreme court. In January 2018, in a 5-4 vote, the prior injunctions were lifted, with the case being allowed to be litigated further in the lower courts.

The judicial branch succeeded in blocking unjust Trump administration policies in the areas of immigration, census questions, DACA, healthcare, and the environment. In June 2020, perhaps in an enlightenment brought by the racial "awakening" of George Floyd protests, the US Supreme Court struck down an act that would allow the termination of LGBT or Q from employment. The same month the Supreme Court upheld DACA, the Obama-era act protecting the children of illegal immigrants from deportation. Chief justice John Robert said Trump failed to "show his work." Again, his legislation was overturned because of the lack of attention to detail.

The tide pool surged, exponentially gathering blue in its tow. The midterm election in 2018 began with a "blue wave." Following a year and a half of reckless partisan policymaking, the enactment and sole intention of which appeared to be in the service of MAGA, red bled to purple, and the VAP turned out in droves. The 2018 mid-term election saw the highest turnout since the 1962 mid-term.

United States Mid-term Elections since 1946

Year	1946	1954	1962	1970	1978
% of VAP	39	43	48	47	39

Year	1986	1994	2002	2010	2018
% of VAP	38	41	39	37	50

Democrats gained forty-one seats in the House of Representatives and control of that body of Congress. It is worth considering that Donald Trump's racism, his xenophobia, his impediment to the progress of the LGBT community, set the bar higher. The backlash was demonstrative. Openly gay and transgender people took House seats and state legislative positions. Ilan Omar (D-MN) and Rashida Tlaib (D-MI) were the first Muslim women elected to Congress. Alexandria Ocasio-Cortez became the youngest female (age twenty-nine) to be elected to Congress. Women pushed at the ceiling more, and the yield was a rise in the percentage of women in Congress. The 116th Congress was 23.7 percent female, up from 20.6 percent in the previous Congressional configuration.

The catastrophe of the 45th president brought out mass frustration, anger, even hatred, which in turn brought out voters who were ultimately offered a lesson in the importance of a mid-term. Whether or not it will be remembered or deemed a necessity to save a Democracy from a bogus president hell-bent on selling it out for his own motives, remains to be seen. The midterm election is the unfiltered direct opportunity for the voting population to have a voice in how well, and by whom, the president is checked and/or balanced. The 2018 election was the highest ever because, quite simply, Donald Trump is the most objectionable president ever elected. It is somewhat of a tell to me that Republicans, for all their vitriol of the Obama presidency, or even the maligning of Bill Clinton (who was no Obama), that they did not vote more. Democrats vote while Republicans lobby and buy elections. As Republicans crony, as they bedfellow with the NRA and porn stars waiting to sign non-disclosure agreements, as bills surmount on Mitch McConnell's desk, the GOP seeps further in the swamp and away from any resemblance of the party of Lincoln, Teddy Roosevelt, or even John McCain. Its voters are looking elsewhere. Fifty-year veteran Republican voters will vote for Biden in 2020, and I can't help thinking that for at least the past four years part of them, a hated part, a fiber they'd fight to the death to admit having, wished they'd voted for anyone but Trump— even Hillary.

* * *

April 22, 2020, marked the fiftieth time we paid homage to the earth. The meandering masked MAGA men and women of Michigan observed Earth Day by protesting orders to stay home. In response to the COVID-19, as the dissipating, virulent, MAGA men and women hang on to their last shred of dignity, as they hold their facemasks and long guns protesting to open the economy to a customer base in quarantine, it hits me. There, on the capitol steps in Lansing, in typical hypocritical fashion, the Republicans march and demonstrate. What is odd about this speculation? Why is it so surreal? What have decades of Democratic marches, protests, sit-ins told history. The left makes use of their tool, their First Amendment right. It is a much less used tool in the right's sparse shed. Although this glib and incredulous protest particularly struck me as a group trying to stay true to ideals they really do not want. When it comes right down to it, when thousands of Americans have died on Trump's watch (which is a pandemic and not a war and should not be allowed to go under the cover of one), when simple logistical math suggests they or a loved one could be one of those deaths, the vast majority of "MAGots" choose life over an economy. That nascent Republican is in there somewhere. The one whose ancestors took pride in belonging to the party of Lincoln, not the party of greed and a good economy above anything, even life itself. They echo Patrick Henry's words of 1775, "Give me liberty, or give me death!" The MAGA protesters hold placards that claim, "Give me liberty or give me COVID-19." It does not have the same conviction. Henry's cry was from a speech that questioned the value of life when it was lived in tyranny (by King George III) knowing that soon many would die in the context of a revolution, a consequence they willingly could expect. Nice try, but a far, muted cry from Henry.

VI. The Logistics of Voting

A football, or the goalposts, are often the metaphors that become enmeshed in the modern political lexicon. To refer to a political football is more than just accepting an issue for the bipartisan nature it has. Each side will run with it, spike it, even exploit it for their own ends. To get more yardage, more space to run, even dance in the end zone, one side moves the goalposts, again, preferably into their end zone. If we extend the metaphor, run with it, the voting landscape becomes a gridiron with intrinsic down makers and foul lines. Voting blocs constantly change and with it the American electorate, the composition of the state legislature, and finally the Electoral College. All in the service of an oblong pigskin. Well, even metaphors have their limits.

In 1812, Governor Elbridge Gerry signed a bill redistricting Massachusetts to favor his Democratic-Republican Party. Long before a football, or its goals, could be moved to satisfy anyone, the governor lent his name to the process. A portmanteau with salamander was created, and it carried on, stifling, obstructing, occasionally orchestrating fair voting practices to the end of time or Democracy, whichever comes first. The basic constitutional constructs have not changed noticeably since 1789, however, the routine politics of American life have, drastically, through history. As one might guess, the legislative branch of government, specifically the House of Representatives, is most vulnerable to gerrymandering. It wants it, needs it, and opens its doors to it usually as a partisan measure. In modern elections, in races for the

House seats, there is generally a low level of competition. Until recent years, the incumbent was likely to dominate the election result. If they run for reelection, they win by often sizable margins. Due to this low contention, the membership in Congress is relatively consistent. Also, partisan seat distribution in that body of Congress is not quick to notice shifts in public preference.

Congressional races of yore were the subjects of much more contention. In the mid-late nineteenth century, such contests were met with fierce partisanship, profound voter interest, peaked turnout, and insidiously high competition. Between 1870 and 1890, almost 45 percent of elections in the House came down to margins of 10 percent or less. Comparatively, only 22 percent of House elections in the 2000s could claim margins that thin. Current elections aside, the fierce competition of district-level Congressional elections in the late 1800s reflected the struggles to control national government, reinforcing them for generations. This meant that ratios in the House of Representatives were subject to marked shifts during the mid-late 1800s. In 1854, for instance, Democrats lost an impressive 74 seats. In a time when the House had only 234 seats, this was a comparable loss at 30 percent. Twenty years later, at the peak of Re-constructional fury, the Republicans suffered a massive loss in the House—giving up a whopping 94 seats! Then, in another twenty years, the Democrats upped the loss to 114 seats—out of a possible 357. Before the twentieth century, to generate this much contention, to produce such vast margins of a popular vote, there was proliferative voter turnout. From 1870 to the turn-of-the-century, when southern Democrats were trying to suppress the votes of black Americans, each party had control of the House precisely half of the time. That trend of intense competition for elected office influenced who ran, weeding out those candidates who decided to be career politicians. Today it is typical for almost 95 percent of incumbents to defend their seat and win. By contrast, in 1852 half of all incumbents sought election and tenures in Congress were much shorter. It was common for a member to serve a couple of terms, at which point they'd return to their home state to perhaps pursue local office, with the satisfaction of a job done to the best of their ability. Turnover was high and incentives, beneficial, political, and monitorial, were fewer. In 1843, less than 30 percent of House members had been in Congress over two years. The job never got old, and tenured Congressmen were the minority. This early fluidity, the disallowance of House structure to grow stale and inflexible in its legislative ways, made the reciprocal by-play required to form such relationships that are needed to make sustainable policy coalitions difficult to materialize.

The nineteenth-century electoral and legislative tenor was what it was. Historians and scholars are divided on the reasons for the sharp disparity between past and contemporary government, the somewhat roguish and tumultuous versus "professionalized" politics. Most theories fall to realignment and critical elections. It is a theory that purports the summation that the American electorate is divided, going through periods of sustained trends of electoral normalcy and then shorter periods in which traditional voting patterns and ideological reliances are subject to dramatic and sudden shifts. A critical election is classified as such because of its abrupt nature, resulting in the irretractable changes in voting patterns. There are marked changes in the turnout of the VAP, usually at the national level, causing battles over nominations, party platforms, and ideological alignments. When an ideological coalition realigns itself, created is a unified majority party able to incite major policy shifts. Elections were held in 1828, 1860, 1896 and 1932 that qualify as critical.

In the general election of 1828, the same candidates from four years earlier vied for the White House. National Republican Party candidate John Quincy Adams, the incumbent, ran against Democratic hopeful Andrew Jackson. Touted as "the common man's candidate," Jackson's election marked a fundamentally democratic shift in the American electoral process. Having lost to him in 1824, Jackson's defeat of Adams marked the beginning of Democratic dominance at the federal level. The election nurtured the idea of "Jacksonian Democracy," a philosophy that gave suffrage to white males over 21, not just property owners. It also restructured several accepted federal institutions. Political models shifted from the First Party System to the Second. As political science perceives it, from roughly 1792 to 1824, control of the presidency, Congress and the states was based on the contesting of two parties: The Democratic-Republican and the Federalist. From 1828 to 1854, the electorate witnessed a higher voter turnout, becoming the grounds for rallies, partisan newspapers, and fierce party loyalties. The two parties of the old system became the Jackson led Democratic party and The Whig Party formed by National Republican Henry Clay and Jackson opponents. In other words, politics grew a face, giving the electorate character, which increased the benefits of voting. More people could vote, and the poorer factions of the populace now had a voice. They now had a voice, a reason to let themselves be heard.

In 1860, Abraham Lincoln filled the Republican ticket with Hannibal Hamlin. Together they ran against southern Democrat James Breckinridge and Joseph Lane in an election that catalyzed the Civil War. The Republican platform directed a policy of no interference with slavery in the states that allowed it but took a stand against its expansion into the new territories. The Republicans nominated Lincoln. The Democrats convened twice that year, the first time failing to offer a nominee. At the second convenience, a senator from Illinois, Stephan Douglas, was nominated to carry the idea of "popular sovereignty," having each territory decide on its slave status. This plan ended up in the alienation of many southern Democrats. With sparse support in the South, Lincoln was able to carve out a plurality of the popular vote, as well as much of the electoral vote. There were divisions in the GOP, chiefly concerning the future of slavery. There were differences that ultimately ensured the party the White House. It was also an election that caused the secession of several southern states and, in April 1861, a battle at Fort Sumter that was the start of the Civil War.

The campaign, which ultimately pitted Republican William McKinley against Democrat William Jennings Bryan, took place during the economic panic of 1893. The election of 1896 can be classified as realigning because it signaled the end of the old, third party system (a historical term used to describe the changes in American nationalism and race during the latter half of the nineteenth century) and began the fourth party system (describing the Republican dominance from 1896 to 1932). Its aligning properties were further amplified by incumbent president Grover Cleveland's declination to seek a second consecutive term, leaving the Democratic field open.

The election in 1932 was won in a landslide victory. More than 57 percent of the popular vote was won by Franklin Roosevelt, governor of New York. FDR's policies resonated with an America mired in the Great Depression, largely a consequence of the fiscally irresponsible policies of the incumbent, Republican Herbert Hoover. Roosevelt's election marked the end of a Republican dominance in the executive branch of government. It moved the needle on the political spectrum to the left, where it would stay (with modest movement) for over three decades.

* * *

In a time before the one person, one vote paradigm, before the Voting Rights Act, state legislators met little resistance when they chose to redistrict. They had free reign in how they changed maps. Every now and then, Congress stepped in to add provisions to the many apportionment acts. They mandated that district populations be made as equal as possible. However, evidence suggests that these Congressional directives were rarely enforced. Other than requiring that districts maintain geographical proportion, the whole process was woefully lacking in any kind of oversight. As a result, the designers of political maps in the nineteenth century had a wider array of demographic levers to pull than contemporary makers do. Thus, when a political party controlled a state government, it was quick to indulge such leverage. Contrary to modern politics, which relies on Congress redrawing boundaries at ten-year intervals, back in the day, adjustments were made at will. Between 1862 and 1896, with a single exception, at least one state redrew its Congressional district boundaries. For instance, Ohio redistricted six times between 1878 and 1890. Barring a federal reapportionment, which added (or subtracted) seats from a state's Congressional delegation, a state could remain years with the same party lines. Connecticut maintained the same lines from 1842 until 1912.

Gerrymandering, its frequency and necessity, evolved. It redrew district lines and then withdrew to redraw again in as many election cycles necessary to wash out a contentious platform plank. The incumbents and career politicians took until the twentieth century to take root in political ground still being cultivated. Before legislators took full advantage of indefinite terms, before love of status benefits and money eclipsed civil service, protecting the incumbent seat was much less of a political caveat than simply garnering as many House seats for your party as possible. It was a full-on partisan advantage, and the designers of their maps whittled the districts into narrow but winnable margins. During much of the 1800s, particularly following the Civil War, it was common to have very thin Congressional divisions in the national vote. This was a time when the movements in the electorate were at their peak, and parties looked elsewhere for an electoral advantage. Redistricting offered that edge. It was a matter of timing when to redistrict, when to opt-out, either of which could mean the majority or minority in a house of Congress. In 1878, earlier Democratic redistricting in Ohio and Missouri allowed that party to retain control of the House. Broad or narrow, timing was everything. In 1888, Republicans orchestrated some last-minute redistricting in Pennsylvania to codify themselves a small majority in the House. Those crafty Republicans, decades before corruption and moral decay set in, they knew how to turn tables on a dime.

The partisan charged, unpredictable nature of redistricting was a decisive factor to the careers of politicians. Contentious districts were drawn, and political careers were abbreviated because of it. Sitting members of Congress faced a greatly varied redistricting schedule, and usually one that was highly partisan. Basically, the partisan redistricting could end a political career. However, the unpredictable nature of congressional redistricting also confounded the ability to plan a long-term career. As a result, the incentives for Congressmen to make investments of time or money in a campaign defending their seat were limited. The frequent rigorous redistricting of the past helps explain the trend that manifested itself as "candidate-centered" politics in the twentieth century. In the modern era, with courts having still not entered the political fray, states were not compelled to reconfigure their district boundaries. The competitive nature in state legislatures for seats declined sharply in the early to mid-1900s. Gone was the incentive to frequently redistrict for a partisan advantage, and many states hung that gerrymander tool back in the political shed until further notice. Legislators embarked on careers in Congress no longer fearing the reaper of frequent and unpredictable redrawing of their districts. This latent longevity in tenure affected the internal power of the House, having repercussions on American politics at the national level. Committee chairmanships were cemented with newfound tenure. The radical changes in the first half of the twentieth century set the stage for the concept that had been waving furtively on the horizon—candidate-centered politics.

* * *

There is only a power struggle when there is no productive alternative, pressure valve, fuse, or scapegoat. The fierce competition for state legislative favor, which in the end translated to an electoral edge, began to wane in its necessity and incentive as soon as the Democratic Party introduced the concept of one person, one vote, party loyalty, rallies, and electoral diversity. By the turn of the nineteenth century, that competition in the legislative branch of government had slowed to a trickle. The frequency in partisan swings and legislative turnover had radically dropped. In one instance, from 1900 until 1960, the majority of the House changed hands a total of seven times. Four of the shifts occurred between 1946 and 1952, that period when Republicans gained the upper hand in the House, only to give it back two years later. For the most part, the Democrats owned the House following the 1930 election. They held the majority, without exception, for 40 years (1954–1994). As noted, the Republican Party can trace its origins to 1854. In 1858 they began their longest ownership of the House, ending in 1878.

Decline in partisan turnover also correlated with the individual member turnover rate. Toward the close of the twentieth century, over 90 percent of sitting House members were seeking (and winning) reelection. Still evolving, the twentieth-century changes in electoral politics set the cornerstones for Congressional politics. Unwavering partisan policies and the stalwarts of legislative careers nurtured the formation of the seniority rules and the committee chairmanships, without which Congress, especially in the Trump-era, would suffer. A fundamental difference of Congress in the modern era is that there is more emphasis on serving, or establishing (sometimes) a rapport with constituents and forming across-the-aisle relationships with colleagues. This modern political "professionalism," the spirited work ethic "for the people" and not what ground needs to be won and for whom, rippled out to other branches of federal government. Bureaucrats, agencies, judges, right up to the presidency, had to temper their conduct to mesh with the modern Congress. But partisan and individual turnover in the House was not sustainable. Even in the early 1900s, it was declining and never fully recovered. The explanation for this twentieth-century antithesis may lie in its recent history. It is argued that, of the four significant elections I cited, the one in 1896 altered voting patterns and partisan alignments, loosening party loyalties. The binary nature of elections, the wins of Republicans in the North, Democrats in the South, resulted in a basic regional politics (hence the red and blue of today). Created was a tenable climate in which incumbent candidates could run for reelection and win at greatly accelerating rates. The districts were safe from malfeasant gerrymanders. Candidates saw an easy win.

Another, less culpable, way to look at the modernization of Congress is the exponential growth of power at the federal level. The enhanced stringency of policy tools available to politicians served to make Washington appear more attractive, somewhere between the partisan vacuum of the nineteenth century and the swampish ecosystem that's cultivated today where integrated politics goes to die. At one time, in a galaxy far, far away, power had a seat in state capitols. Over time, an integration of the federal economy and the subjective role of the federal government in orchestrating that economy began its transformation from a kind of wizard behind the curtain (to whom states were implored to pay little attention) to a seat of power. Gerrymandering played an integral part in bringing forth the so-termed professionalism that has sustained Washington so well. Partisan politics has made a comeback in the twenty-first century. For the first seven years of the twenty first century, the Republicans controlled the House of Representatives, ceding it back to the Democrats in 2007, for Democrats to hold for most of Barack Obama's presidency. Republicans controlled the House, and then the Senate, for many of the Obama years and the beginning of Trump's term. In 2018, with a net gain of 41 seats, the Democrats took back majority rule in one house of Congress.

There is a nature and nurture effect, a political science. There is a nature, a human reaction, and accepted and even expected behavior to how people will vote, what candidates they support, and what issues get credence. Nature is beholden to a status quo, what has gone before, and what has evolved to take vastly differing approaches by Republicans and Democrats. Nurture derails the science. It upsets the status quo. The 1960s, for example, were the stage for a lot of political nurturing. The nation grew, changed, painfully, and the call for nurturing was omnipresent throughout the decade and into the next. Redistricting, gerrymandering, in the modern era, gave rise to legislative prowess in 1962. The US Supreme Court heard a case that year brought by Charles Baker from Shelby County, Tennessee. Baker intended to sue the secretary of state, Joe Carr, because Tennessee had not been redistricted since the 1900 Census. Baker's district, comprising the city of Memphis, had experienced almost ten times the growth in population as rural districts in the sixty years, districts that maintained equal representation in the state legislature. In a 6-2 decision, the high court ruled in favor of Baker, establishing the practice (and authority) of courts to settle such issues. This decision contradicted the previous acceptance that courts lacked the competence to weigh such questions. Two years later, in Supreme Court cases *Wesberry v. Sanders* and *Reynolds v. Simms*, the Constitution was nurtured. It was found that redistricting was required by each state following every decennial census. The decision also stipulated that equal population be provided in state legislative districts pertaining to their Congressional seats. For example, Minnesota's Congressional districts correspond to its electoral votes (ten) to be in proportion with the population in individual districts. The US Senate, however, was exempt from this ruling.

American politics evolves, at times ruefully, through history, most often through the willful nature of its beasts. Our Constitution, a Declaration of Independence, exist as documents slated to conflate and confound the ideas of nature and nurture, the inherent fortitude of man (and then woman) to act politically. They distort and import, from generation to generation, providing the carrot in front of the ass. They supply the eternal superlatives that no doubt was quilled with the best of intentions, the lofty visions of defectors of a monarchy steeped in the fated idea of one man, one vote. Righteous, superficial promises made will, in due time, fade into political lexicons. There they are subject to generational (or even election cyclical) change and become talking points or, better yet, narratives (civil rights) that provide political nutrition.

By the latter half of the twentieth century, the political landscape was teetering on a redistricting revolution. Humans become slaves to their ideologies, their parties, and ultimately pigeon-hole themselves. They taunt the tenacious nature of the political beast, almost always banging the drum to revolt with righteous intent. Bounded by party lines and the chance to manipulate the opposing party, redistricting is inevitable. It seeks to change the disparity of several social issues, among them the rural-urban relationship, racial discrimination, and agricultural versus the industrial grounds for the economy. Prior to *Baker v. Carr*, many states in regions other than the segregated South went decades without redistricting. In fact, the court was usually reluctant to get involved in districting issues, emphasizing its hands-off approach in the 1946 case *Colegrove v. Green*. In that case, the Illinois state legislature had failed, like Tennessee, to redistrict since the 1900 census. Half a century passed, and much of the Illinois population resides in the greater Chicago area. The concentrated groups of potential voters from the South settling in other regions of the country are the result of migration that began in 1870. The first wave consisted of a "New Immigration" from southern and eastern Europe. American cities in the north and western US grew, from roughly 1880 until 1915, at which point WWI halted the trend. A second wave began of mostly southern blacks moving north and west to cities like New York, Los Angeles and Detroit. They sought economic opportunities as well as legal and political equality. By the mid-1940s—due to a third wave of white Americans moving from small towns to big cities—the nation was an urban society. Because of the lapse in drawing of political boundaries for much of the first half of the twentieth century, the migrations of people, the voting power of those blocs in expanding regions was numerically diluted while the largely white rural voting blocs was in turn enhanced. The result was that state legislatures were mostly dominated by rural interests. Concessions were not made to reach district proportions equal to their population. Prior to the twentieth century, the members in the US House of Representatives fluctuated with populations. The House grew with greater population and lost seats with stable or shrinking populations. In 1911, due to the resistance to reapportionment in the House, Congress voted to fix the number of seats at 435. Opposition to reapportionment had some adverse effects. Cook County, which comprises Chicago, was paying 53 percent of Illinois taxes, making the economic importance of the city to Illinois economy dwarf its representation in the state legislature. This oversight began the political corruption in the twentieth century for which Chicago is known. Voters were left with money as a political cudgel to find proportion to their legislative representation. In 1946, the discrepancy prompted political journalist John Gunther to write, "the only way Chicago can operate in the legislature at all is to try to buy it." Rural residents, as well as lawmakers, feared ultimate surrender. They feared Chicago, with its broad shoulders, its burgeoning size, its global hog butchering status, with wide disproportions socially, culturally, and racially. The smaller contingency of rural white voters feared ultimately having to cede their legislative power to the economic power of urban Chicago.

It only became more unbalanced and unequal in time, setting the bumpy course for Chicago's political future. In the 1930s and 40s, it became a major Democratic stronghold in the context of FDR's New Deal. The outlying areas of Illinois, however, remained in the "Land of Lincoln." Rural areas maintained an allegiance to the Republican Party, as did many states in the north and west of America. Later in the twentieth century redistricting came to mean that, in addition to transferring power to migrants to the bigger cities, there was a transfer of legislative control from Republicans to Democrats. At the height of the New Deal, in Illinois going north and west into the nation, power at the national level belonged to Democrats, and the last vestiges of GOP control were state governments—and they fought hard to maintain it. The Republicans had farming. They had the value it brought to the economies of Illinois and the north and west of the country. Following 1870, though, there was a gradual decline in the farming population. The volume of the crops and their dollar value remained much the same. The result was that a greater volume of agricultural products was produced by a diminished workforce. After the 1930s, redistricting presented a situation in which farm interests were likely to be undercut or not represented at all in the general assembly as far as agriculture's economic importance in the state. It was the effective exchange of the cities under-representation of economic goods for the rural areas, the result of which was the discouragement of redistricting. The severity of the shifts in power, how drastic they were, and the time it took to balance, was contingent on how long a state waited to redistrict. A basic inability, or unwillingness, on the part of state legislatures to address the problem of urban under-representation proliferated, along with efforts to end segregation in the South. This prompted the US Supreme Court to render decisions like Baker and other relevant cases. When the courts did finally intervene on matters of gerrymandering, justices of the day were acutely aware that they were making decisions that would have a lasting impact on the shape of politics. Chief Justice Earl Warren commented that the Baker case was maybe the most important of his time on the court (1954–69).

* * *

Article I, section II of the US Constitution pertains to the census. Its third clause argues the idea that for a government of the people to function, those people must be counted. What a concept. The Founders wanted an "enumeration" to take place within three years of the first Congress. After this, for the rest of the time, or until the experiment failed, the enumeration should occur "every Term of ten Years, in such Manner as they by law shall direct." This decennial tally went on mostly unabridged for over two centuries, until 2018. In April, the Trump administration, with their partisan motives, suggesting the addition of the intrusive question "Is this person a citizen of the United States?" to the census. The query found its origins in the somnolent mind of Commerce Secretary Wilbur Ross. The question was criticized by former Census Bureau directors from each party, before being found unconstitutional by multiple federal judges. In the words of the Constitution, the census is supposed to enumerate all *people* of the United States, not only citizens. Less than eight percent of the people residing in the US are non-citizens, leaving a higher percentage—about fourteen—of people who maintain households with non-citizens.

A respected scientist at the Census Bureau, John Abowd, argued that Secretary Ross's citizenship question would serve as a deterrent to no less than 630,000 households from completing the census, the result of which would have been that an estimated 6.5 million people were not counted. The implications would be determinative to voting. The Congressional seating chart is determined by the census. The distribution of those seats correlates to the Electoral College. An accurate census also determines where trillions in federal dollars go, and an undercount could mean an entire state, or an ethnic community could not get needed federal appropriations. The census, it would appear, is a mirror of our politics, reflective of the promise and prejudices of a nation. In each census, the first three words of the Constitution are probed for their intrinsic value, the mirror image that vanishes frequently, never so much as during the Trump administration. Like a question asked in an exponentially rhetorical patter, it is asserted, who, then, are the people of "We the people?"

Well, the question once had its value. The people counted for something, if for only that—to be counted, enumerated, with grave precision. The Founders, a fickle group of celebrated colonials, all agreed that an accurate count of potential participants was an essential component of a government, especially one aiming to be self-governing with democratic aspirations. Only after we declared our independence from King George did anyone really care who lived here in the colonies. In monarchal days, mere estimates of the population were sufficient. For example, in 1714, King George I figured that there were 375,000 white and 58,000 black subjects living in the American colonies. Native Americans likely dwarfed those populations combined, but they were not subjects and therefore not counted. By 1776 the population had swelled to 2.75 million white and .5 million black Americans. After the war, the job of enumeration became more difficult. Filled with the wanderlust independence creates, Americans were constantly migrating westward to find their fortune. Keeping an accrued count of them proved much harder than when they saved in thirteen colonies. After all, they were moving west, away from the government and the taxes it represented to them. Keeping an accurate count of African Americans also became a challenge for the fledgling government. According to the Articles of Confederation, the document preceding the Constitution, Southern states were all too happy to number the enslaved in their populations. Doing so bolstered their electoral strength in Congress. It was not a blanket win situation. If counting the odd slave added on a federal tax to the population, for instance, it was not in a state's best interest to report them. Whether the compromise reached was detrimental to the future of democracy is a matter of hindsight, but it was written into the Constitution to preserve the Union. The African Americans were counted as "three-fifths of all other persons." Thus, was created a fortuitous arrangement that augmented the voice of southern states in Congress while also allowing the spread of slavery to virtually fly under the radar until the Civil War.

The census provided a way of grounding vagabonds. On the first Monday in August 1790, an invasive procedure began, a decennial ritual. United States marshals dispersed their forces throughout America, collecting data on its populous. States did not always readily provide the required information. Some, notably Rhode Island and South Carolina, proved more problematic than most. At the completion of that inaugural census, the findings were not even published for public consumption. They were posted, I surmise, like a flyer or auction posting "at two of the most public places. . . to remain for the inspection of all concerned." Nearly eighteen months ended with the headcount of roughly 4,000,000 people, elevating membership in the House of Representatives from 65 to 105. The French, who had helped win independence for America, were impressed with the timely institution of the census. A statistician referred to the United States as "a people who instituted the statistics of their country on the very day when they founded their government, and who regulated by the same instrument the census of inhabitants, their civil and political rights, and the destinies of the nation." (It probably sounded more flattering in the original French). The curve became slippery, and more questions accompanied each census. Its origin changed location as well. By 1849, it was no longer the responsibility of the State Department and fell to the Department of Interior. The DOI had become so much of an amalgamation of random duties that it had earned the appellation "The Great Miscellany." The census that was conducted in 1850 for the first time tracked the perpetually mobile people in California, for example, as it was a recent acquisition of the union. It must have been impressive that year to find America had quite handily usurped the population of their former captors. The US could boast a population of 23,191,876, over 8,000,000 more inhabitants than England. There was divinity (and a whole lot of procreation) at work, and size mattered to citizens of the new nation. It was Manifest Destiny, and America could have been even bigger if Founders and their descendants had gotten along with its original inhabitants.

Following the Civil War's Union victory, the three-fifths rule was off the record, for less than practical purposes. Suddenly able to enumerate their population wholly, southern states retained a political lever from the rule. Language in the Fourteenth Amendment ensures that allotment of House seats was to be determined by "the whole number of persons in each State," an idea that has been upheld by the Supreme Court since its writing. In 1870 and 1880, the census continued, increasingly becoming a Herculean task for civil servants. Some years the interim was consumed figuring the results, and one census bled to the next. It became ad nausea, with one question providing a context in which the next was valid:

1) State; county; town

   a) What proportion of the land devoted to grain; raising is

      i) hilly?

      ii) rolling?

      iii) level, alluvial or bottom land?

   b) What is the prevailing kind of soil (as clay, loam, alluvial, black prairie, etc.)?

   c) What is the character of the subsoil?

   For the 1890 census, the Bureau began to investigate methods for a faster tabulation. An invention of a former census worker, Herman Hollerith, was selected by the Bureau in 1888. He had an electric tabulating machine that used punch cards with printed symbols to categorize data, in this case, the findings of who made up America. Holes on the long cards represented every facet of the census, national origin, age, marital status, and so forth. With Hollerith's machine, the most private points of a person's identity were suddenly subjects to be noted and calibrated. In the upper left of the card, a citizen's race was spelled out symbolically: W–white, B–black, Mu–mulatto, Qd–quadroon, and Oc–octoroon Americans. The machine's efficiency only led to more questions. The experienced tabulator was able to process 80 punch cards a minute. The technology led to the most detailed reading of America to date by the turn of the nineteenth century producing a 21,410-page document.

Decades from any kind of digital storage, Hollerith was left with the problem of storing all the paper his machines produced. For the first wave of censuses (1790–1880), data collected was bound into books that amounted to 4,957 volumes. The 1890 census, five times bigger than the combined data, was obviously more than a book could hold. It required over a mile of shelf space to house, and so the data sat, adjacent to the grumbles of the officials charged to guard it as it mounted. It was too big to be copied, the one existing copy flowing into multiple buildings—the US Patent Office and the Pension Bureau. Some relief came in 1913 when it was moved to the basement storage of a new Commerce Building. Papers were wrapped in twine, given narrow pine shelves in a boiler room. Who can guess what became of early census records? Give that reader a cigar.

One January afternoon in 1921, an employee noticed smoke. Investigators thought that maybe the census records were the victims of spontaneous combustion. A salient lesson came out of the likely turn of events, one of man's willful culpability and the fortuitous flammability of guilt with history. A government was now confronted with its weak affinity to protect, or even preserve, its past. A responsibility was there, lying in a pile of slightly charred papers telling the first real story of America. Two documents of major importance—the Declaration of Independence and the Constitution—were kept in a wooden filing cabinet at the State Department. To better protect these frequently referenced tools of governments, a National Archive was created. Parched and withered, the partial 1890 census remained in a brewery for the next decade. They were eventually, intentionally, destroyed in 1933.

For the twenty-fourth time in America's history, a census was conducted in 2020. With the Trump administration's denominative question posed, it was one of the most contested, surely the most digitalized. Hollerith would likely have jumped at the chance to himself procure such efficient apps and online facilitations. Although, as innovators and visionaries should well know, from Steve Jobs to Bill Gates, with technology come inherent risks. Even Hollerith, whose tabulating machine amazed a generation at the cusp of the twentieth century, eventually had his technology bought by IBM, who contracted with the Third Reich during WWII. But there have been many more recent incidents of this fantastic digital world opening a backdoor to adverse effectiveness. Wikileaks and the Russian hacking in the 2016 election or the highly problematic app that delayed greatly the final tally of the 2020 Democratic caucus in Iowa. Technology specifically made for the census has failed elsewhere in the world. In 2016 a high-tech design for taking the census failed in Australia. The US Census Bureau is not well funded, way down on the list of things for which the Trump administration cuts funding, and innovative methods of taking it are rarely given a dry run. In figuring the 2019 budget, the Administration advised Congress to create a $4,000,000 deficit in its allocation for the census—$4,000,000 less than they spent in 2009.

History is a record, often broken, but nonetheless encouraged to play. Enticed by the want of something better, more radical (less reactionary), we follow the Founders' wishes reluctantly like a last will and testament. They worked on the assumption that self-governing might invite some self-understanding. They figured that accounting for every citizen in the Union could be no less than a matter of principle, and if in 1790 George Washington's administration had paused to consider the monumental task before it or to devote time and resources to more pressing issues, no one would have been overly critical. But the decennial enumeration is done perhaps with the solace that it needs to be done only every tenth year. Still, it is a recurring reflection of who we are, a record of how we change in 3,652-day increments.

* * *

In 2016, a diverse spectrum of blue-collar workers gathered at their local poll in Flint, Michigan. Enough of those workers held their nose and voted for Donald Trump to give him an electoral victory in that state, an action many would silently rue for the next four years. They fell for the bait, the promise of jobs in their sustaining auto industry, his ugly American venom and red meat patter, or his sympathies to a pro-life audience (a greater hypocrisy does not exist). The working-class in Michigan that year was widely underestimated, showing overwhelming support for a Republican when the demographic was known to vote Democratic. Trump won the sixteen electoral votes. As for the popular vote, there was a .23 percent margin in Michigan. What did they get out of it, a few months of vindication? A brief vantage point from which they were heard by people likely also holding their noses, soon to be holding their heads in hand, realizing what their little outburst had wrought? Maybe though, it was not all for naught. Maybe something good could come of an otherwise disastrous yen that would leave an indelible mark on the collective consciences (and collars) of a margin of working-class voters in Michigan and other swing states Trump won in 2016. The pattern of an election learns its course through the veins of American. It thrives with the vanity of the electorate. In 2016 there were sufficient voters to comprise an electorate that ignored common sense. They willfully invited a nominee who, by any elementary intellect, would prove to be corrupt, to sit in the highest office in America. The electorate hit rock bottom. It scraped the DC swamps and dredged up the creature who, ironically, pitched himself as the one to drain them. (I guess in a way he did, and we see what crawled out). We have nowhere to go but up. As an eternal optimist, one who sees the swamp as half empty, the 2016 election may well have changed the electorate. . .for the better.

In 2006 New Mexico was first on the road to a trend in demographics likely to shape America for the foreseeable future. Its VAP crossed that juncture from being majority white to "majority/minority." It is a broadening of the electorate that spread to California and then Texas by 2019. In 2016, minorities accounted for about 38 percent of the US population. This number is expected to rise, by demographers (at least as optimistic as I tend to be), to more than fifty by 2044. Close on its heels will be the voting age population. For years, perhaps decades, after 2016, the electorate was predicted to change drastically in favor of minorities. In states such as California, New Mexico, and Hawaii, which have never had a white majority, minorities are predicted to make up as much as 75 percent of the VAP by 2060. Conversely, white bred states like Maine, Vermont, or New Hampshire don't have a shot at even breaking 15 percent in the next four decades.

The electorate is changing radically, repositioning itself in the throes of the Trump election and the ensuing anguish, much like a docile dog shakes off an infestation of fleas. It may be coincidental, and one could argue that change would have happened with or without Trump, although there is nature and nurture. This change in the electorate is definitely a result of the latter. Trump's acerbic policies kneaded democracy, tendering narratives that had gone to the political landfill of complacency, or even apathy. The shock factor to the electorate alone was enough to jolt the system to move in a progressive manner that otherwise would take at best two moderate Republican and Democratic administrations to achieve. It is true, what does not kill us will make us stronger (in 2020, no longer hyperbole). If there is any vestige of America, an electorate, or a democracy left when Trump leaves office tranquilized, it will be stronger. It will be changed for the better, or at least face a future less resistant to change. The electorate now belongs to the next generation. The Gen-Xs and millennials populate the VAP. Our parents taught us how to vote. Born when blacks were hosed and bombs fell on the yellow people on the other side of the world, we grew up with a disgust, a feeling for the pointlessness of war and separation of races. Generation X passed those ideas to their kids. The baby-boomers fought that war, and now they are dying out, literally, at a faster rate in the age of COVID-19 and, more poignantly, COVID-19 under the egregious dereliction of the Trump administration. In 1982, baby-boomers made up almost 50 percent of the electorate. In 2016, like the millennials, they accounted for a little less than a third. It is predicted that by 2060 they will have all but died out, merely a faint image of the face they now pose at Trump in spastic contortions. If any configuration, any random population, of Americans is left by 2060, roughly a tenth of an electorate will belong to generation X, the oldest of whom will be in their 90s. The remaining electorate composition will be split amongst the millennials and their successors, Y and Z. In the interim, for roughly the next forty years, a third of the electorate will be maintained by the millennials.

It took the erratic, incompetent, malicious, divisiveness of a Donald Trump, a jolt to the status quo of the American electorate.

It took the ultimate revulsion of a plurality of the GOP, the steady erosion of basic democratic ideals embraced by each party, to change the course of voting in America. The presidential election of 2020 is America's last chance to save democracy and save for the limitations presented by COVID-19, the voter suppression tactics, that election absolutely must have the highest percentage of the VAP turnout to date. We can also expect, as precedented in 2018, the most diverse electorate and resulting elections. The guarded optimism of a swamp half-empty sees the Democrats winning back the Senate as well as the White House, an occurrence that could break two ceilings: a black female vice president.

* * *

There exists an incongruency in democracy, willfully imposed in bipartisan acceptance for decades. It can boost a party's vote, as well as unfairly render it all but mute in legislatures. The Electoral College is in the first articles of the Constitution. It has its detractors, voters who would like to see its elimination for a more direct election system. Winner-take-all is the normal voting method in forty-eight states. Since 1996, Maine and Nebraska have been the only states not to use the method of electing its state and federal officials. In "WTA," the candidate who wins the popular vote is awarded all a state's electoral votes. California, as an extreme example of the partisan voice WTA can give, all its fifty-five electoral votes go to the popular candidate. Largely Democratic in policy, in governance, and legislature. Its current governor, Gavin Newsome, is a Democrat, as was his predecessor, Jerry Brown. Preceding Brown was Arnold Schwarzenegger, a quite moderate Republican who succeeded Democrat Gray Davis. For over a decade, California has elected governors with liberal ideas. As of February 2019, 19,978, 449 people were registered to vote in California. This made up 79.09 percent of the state's VAP. Of the registered voters, 43.11 percent were Democrats with 23.57 registering as Republicans. In the 2016 election, 61.73 percent of Californians voted for Clinton, with 31.62 percent going for Trump. Winning the popular vote by a margin of 4,269,978 votes, all of California's fifty-five electoral votes went to Clinton. Alternatively, in predominantly red Nebraska, where the winner does not take all, Trump won 58.75 percent of the popular vote to Clinton's 33.70. Trump still won all the state's five electoral votes. However, in Maine, the popular votes went to three candidates: Clinton (47.83 percent), Trump (44.87 percent), and Libertarian Gary Johnson (5.09 percent). Clinton did not take all of Maine's four electoral votes, though. One went to Trump. Maine usually is the most Republican voting state on the eastern seaboard, having voted Democratic only three times; 1912,1964, and 1968. Regarded once as a Republican state, Maine is now safe blue territory, having been lost by George W. Bush in each of his campaigns. As an indication of how red Maine once was, Trump is only the second Republican (after Bush) to win the White House after losing the state. A Democrat has won Maine's popular vote in every presidential election since 1988. One can see how the WTA method used in elections can have its subsequent advantages for a liberal agenda, or Republican, as the case may be. The practice of awarding electoral votes in Maine, based on Congressional districts, began in 1972. That year incumbent Republican Richard Nixon defeated George McGovern in a landslide, beginning five consecutive Republican wins in Maine. In 1992, Bill Clinton ended the streak, leading the state to favor Democrats ever since. As one of the two states not subscribing to WTA rules in voting, Maine split its four electoral votes in 2016, awarding one to Trump (who lost the popular vote) and three to Clinton. An electoral split had not occurred in Maine since the 1828 election of Democrat Andrew Jackson.

Heavily Republican North Dakota got 61.29 of its VAP to vote, with more than half going for Trump. As the winner of the popular vote, he was, of course, entitled to all three electoral votes. The state has voted Republican solidly, only going blue in the landslides of Johnson in 1964 and Franklin Roosevelt in 1932 and 1936. North Dakota is a winner-take-all state with one of the lowest populations in the country at just over 760, 000. It is a statistically red stronghold, barring a Republican who has, or is expected to, bring significant hardship to the country. In Roosevelt's first landslide victory in 1932, he ran against an incumbent, Herbert Hoover, who had led America into the Great Depression with his economy, with a recklessness that has been compared to Trump. In 1964 Johnson ran against Arizona senator Barry Goldwater, a conservative extremist whose feared proximity to the nuclear button was also mentioned during the 2016 campaign with regards to Trump's. That said, it would not surprise me if North Dakota broke rank again and went blue in 2020.

2016 US Presidential Election in North Dakota

Candidate	Popular vote	Electoral vote	Percentage
Donald Trump	216, 794	3	62.96
Hillary Clinton	93, 758	0	27.23
Gary Johnson	21, 434	0	6.22

It's as red as North Dakota and twice as populous, but not bound by law to give its popular candidate all its five electoral votes. Over 70 percent of its VAP turned out to vote in 2016, over half for Trump. Along with Maine, Nebraska uses the so-called Congressional district method in awarding electoral votes. Since the policy began in 1992, Nebraska has split the votes once in 2008, giving Barack Obama the votes in Omaha's districts, and John McCain the remainder of the state. Obama won 41.60 percent of the popular vote, capturing the 2nd Congressional District comprising Omaha and its suburbs. Nebraska's strength as a red state reads much like North Dakota, weakening only because of extremely damaging conservative presidents or candidates. They also went blue in 1964 and 1932.

2016 US Presidential Election in Nebraska

Candidate	Popular vote	Electoral vote	Percentage
Donald Trump	495, 961	5	58.7
Hillary Clinton	284, 494	0	33.7

Currently, both states are governed by Republicans who take cues from Trump in handling the COVID-19 pandemic. Each has refused to put any shelter-in-place orders into effect, with Nebraska determined to keep open a meatpacking plant despite the viral concerns of its workers. They are beginning to see the insanity in not following the social distancing most of the nation has, ignoring Trump and his abject failure to show any kind of leadership or initiative, or even concern, in this crisis. North Dakota, though, I am not as optimistic of their ultimate enlightenment simply because they are not heavily populated, lacking the density of people for which this virus has such an affinity. They are not seeing the cases or death rates that many red states are that are forcing governors' sanity and medial understanding of biology to prevail.

* * *

States choose their party. They identify with it. Candidates campaign with it in mind. The method of casting votes, how, and to whom they are awarded, appears to have little effect on that choice. It didn't in the past, but evidence (like Democrats winning in Maine) suggests the need to reconsider the winner-take-all method of awarding a state's electoral votes. Adherents to the Constitution argue WTA is unfair and could work to the advantage of either party. It is working for Democrats in Massachusetts. This is a state with forty senators from forty districts, the majority of whom are Democrats. If the state's predominantly Democratic legislature passed a law ruling that the state Senate should be elected in a partisan vote in a statewide election, it would most certainly be unconstitutional. The result would be the effectual and intentional removal of a half-million Republican votes, virtually silencing the GOP. Good god. A few years of silence from the upper one percent might be in the better interest of a "Democracy," although it would, quite paradoxically, be undemocratic. And there it is, the catch-22, the reason to vote for better, the pigeon-holed button that's kept the 99 percent fighting for over two centuries.

The Supreme Court does acknowledge the inequities of WTA, having ruled against the implementation of "multimember" districts if it facilitates the prevention of racial minority voting blocs from getting a fair shake in state legislatures. It made the same ruling as it applies to political minorities. Even so, many states want to get rid of WTA as a method of awarding electoral votes, of ensuring statistically that their state will be bound to vote along a defined party line. They make three arguments against its use:

- Winner-take-all has been in use for a long time, a fact only compounding the urgency to rectify a constitutional violation.

- Winner-take-all pre-dates the "one person, one vote" cases that reached the Supreme Court in the 1960s, deciding against other long-established electoral systems. Winner-take-all needs to be given such consideration.

- Winner-take-all does not emulate one person, one vote due to its equal count of every vote. A high electoral count such as California consists obviously of votes by voters from each party, Republican and Democrat. Each is in the pool, competing for all the state's electoral votes.

There is no allowance for the concept of vote dilution, the possible existence of those undercutting multimember districts. The losing party, despite having perhaps millions of votes, gets virtually zero representation. It is a power grab by the dominant party and should be seen for what it constitutes, for what such a system enables, an unfair systemic siphoning of minority voting rights. States wanting to abolish WTA recognize that it is typically not the courts' role to intervene in electoral matters. However, it is also their duty to interpret and enforce the Constitution. WTA is not in the Constitution and, therefore, unconstitutional. There is a reason for judicial intervention. There exist provisions in the Constitution that gives Congress the power to regulate states. No such allowance is, however, preferred, or inferred, from the Elector Clause. Article I, section 4 of the Constitution gives state legislatures the discretion to hold elections of senators and Representatives at the "times, places, and manner" of their choosing. It also states that Congress may at any time, by law, make amendments to those choices. This clause establishes two things. It eliminates any ambiguity in the division of responsibility as it pertains to how federal Senators and Representatives are elected. Basically, such responsibility rests with the states who are under the power of Congress. In addition, the clause stipulates that the power to regulate said elections lie with the corresponding legislative branches of state and federal government, not the executive or judicial.

The electoral system is vulnerable to intemperate, even hostile, change by a partial party. For this reason, among others, it is necessary for the courts to mediate in the removal, the definitive banishment, of the winner-take-all method of electing state and federal officials. Its elimination from the political tapestry of forty-eight states would come as a benefit to all voters. Its dismissal as a partisan tool would essentially make every state battleground fare. The attention to each states' voters would flourish, producing high turnout of VAP as they see how their vote matters as never before. It was the case, for each party, in Massachusetts and Texas, as they were indelibly blue and red, respectively.

William Weld, former governor of Massachusetts, Libertarian running mate to Gary Johnson in 2016, ran as a Republican against the incumbent president. He sees winner-take-all as unconstitutional and gives himself as an example of how it ensures a partisan vote. In his Democratic state of Massachusetts (that does currently have a Republican governor), his chances to win the state in a general election would be slim to none. In 2016 Clinton took all the state's eleven electoral votes as the winner of 60.01 percent of the popular vote, almost twice that of Trump. One must go back to the 1984 shellacking of Walter Mondale by Ronald Reagan to find a general election where a Republican won the state.

1980 US Presidential Election in Massachusetts

Candidate	Popular vote	Electoral vote	Percentage
Ronald Reagan	1,310,936	13	51.22
Walter Mondale	1,239,606	0	48.43

Even here though, the Democrat came closer to beating the spread than any Republican in the next thirty-two years of election cycles. In most of the elections between 1980 and 2016, the Democratic candidate wins by a significantly wider margin of popular votes. In 1980, although distilled some by third-party candidate John Anderson, Democratic incumbent Jimmy Carter lost Massachusetts to former California governor (and Democrat) Reagan by 3,829 popular votes. It is thought that Anderson, a liberal Republican Congressman who ran as an Independent after failing to get the Republican nomination, was a large factor contributing to Reagan's winning the state. Massachusetts has been tilted to the left since 1928 and a Democratic lock since 1960. In the 1972 election, when incumbent Richard Nixon won every other state in the union, including his Democratic opponent's home state of South Dakota, George McGovern won Massachusetts. Reagan's 1980 win was the first time a Republican won all the state's electoral votes since Eisenhower's landslide reelection in 1956.

LBJ's time may be here

In March 2018, former Congressman Beto O'Rourke won the Democratic nomination in Texas with 61.8 percent of the primary vote. He began his campaign for the US Senate against the Republican incumbent Ted Cruz. O'Rourke lost to Cruz by a margin of 2.6 percent. He did set a record for the most votes won by a Democrat in Texas history with 4,000,000, marginally more than Hillary Clinton received in 2016. In the exposing light of Immigration reform, the Trump administration's callous, self-indulgent response to the August 2019 El Paso shooting, and the current exacerbation of COVID-19 cases by a governor insistent to fall in step with Trump's zeal to "open the country," Texas will likely turn blue, at least for the 2020 election. I see swing states in the reliably red South, even Florida, whose importance to an election Tim Russert thought bore repeating three times, going blue. They will go blue, change the electoral page of America, simply because three and a half years of the Trump brand of Republicanism has insulted, frustrated, infuriated, and disgusted so many. It has been allowed to erode away the very foundation of America, the core principles introduced 231 years ago by Thomas Jefferson, James Madison, even the Federalist in the room Alexander Hamilton, whom I see as eighteenth-century iteration of the upper one percent. If Donald Trump's divisiveness has done anything other than worsen hate, it is to reveal how much we are the same. It reveals how, fundamentally, Republicans and Democrats want the same thing. They just differ on how to get there.

* * *

How states have voted in the past tells a story worth noting. It tells their present, future, and their value to the country. It tells what a candidate can most likely expect, whether it is a "swing" or a "safe" state, or if it is even worth their campaign time and expense. A state's voting trends, it's electoral history, with the various reasons that pale in their trivial nature as democracy advances in their spite, is really quite a compelling story.

Minnesota has its DFL (Democratic-Farmer-Labor) enclave in its third, fourth, and fifth Congressional districts. The red bleeds out beyond these borders, however, down south and up north on the iron range where the red stains one's feet. I fear I developed a false sense of security growing up as I did in the sky-blue bosom of the DFL. I carried proudly the instinct that extravagantly Republican ideas would have a hell of a fight in our legislature, and we would certainly never let one win our ten electoral votes. Hillary Clinton won Minnesota with a 1.52 percent margin, too close for comfort, really. Repulsed by the malice and ineptitude of the Trump presidency, the total vacancy of any ability or willingness to even learn to do the job, or even accept the opinion of those who can, it is unlikely Minnesota will come anywhere close to giving a Republican their electoral votes in 2020.

California has an interesting electoral history, with its deep pockets of inflammable red sunk in what, in modern history, has been a bastion of liberalism. One must go back to the shellacking of Michael Dukakis by George H. W. Bush in 1988 to find a red win in the state. Former governor Reagan won the state in both elections, with 1984 capturing the most votes in the state since anti-Catholic sentiment for Al Smith resulted in a win for Republican Herbert Hoover. Winner-take-all is at peak efficiency in its limiting effect in a state this big, with fifty-three districts. For California's delegation in the current 116th Congress, there are forty-six Democrats (including Speaker Pelosi) and 7 Republicans (including House minority leader Kevin McCarthy). In 2000, prompted by the census and article I, section 4 of the Constitution, the California State Legislature was obligated to undergo redistricting for the House of Representatives as well as the California General Assembly. What resulted was a bipartisan gerrymandering in which lines were drawn in such a way as to favor one or the other party. In such configurations, the smaller districts obviously did not compete with the same ferocity and subsequently did not gain equal representation. In 2005, Republican governor Arnold Schwarzenegger proposed entrusting the task of redistricting to retired judges. He called a special election in June that year and placed his proposal on the ballot as proposition 77. The initiative failed overwhelmingly. A California Redistricting Citizens Commission certified district maps in 2011, which went into effect for the 2012 general election in which Obama won over 60 percent of the state. Districts changed. They were no longer reliably red or blue, increasingly taking on a more purple hue. They were no longer safe in composition, as in previous elections, and an incumbent legislator could no longer expect his or her reelection to be a lock. California's size, its districts, its demographic populations all are self-defeating. It is historically Democratic and will likely never be able to have a Republican base with enough political strength to significantly move the needle from the left.

Florida, Florida, Florida. It is the peninsular state to which general elections trickle down. Donald Trump won both the state's twenty-nine electoral votes and 4,617,886 popular votes, defeating Clinton by a narrow (112,911 vote) margin. Florida is diverse enough in minorities, with a high VAP turnout (83 percent in 1992), to make it the country's best indicator of the winner. Incidentally, when Florida backed George H. W. Bush in 1992, it was the first time they'd backed the loser since 1960 when Richard Nixon beat John Kennedy in the state. The election in 1992, in which Clinton carried thirty-two states plus DC, was significant because it marked the beginning of the end of Florida being a reliable red state. It was well on its way to becoming the divided "swing" state we know today. Votes were liable to swing either way. Four years earlier, Bush had won Florida by an even greater margin, making it his runner-up for wins in the South (home state advantage earned H. W. 55.95 percent of Texas). There are similarities with Ohio's voting history, also considered a pivotal swing state, and 1992 was the only election since 1944 that Florida did not vote the same way. Bill Clinton turned at least three counties, many with ethnic populations, Democratic in 1992, and they have voted that way ever since. To find a time when any of the south Florida counties backed a Democrat, one must go back to the state's "Solid South" days when Franklin Roosevelt won all Florida's sixty-seven counties in 1944.

Swing states can then be thought of as some consolation prize to the opponents of WTA. The votes in a state can favor either party's candidate. In recent years states considered to be swing, with a greater likelihood of being in contention, are CO, IA, FL, MI, MN, NV, NH, NC, OH, PA, VA and WI. The two non-WTA states, Maine and Nebraska, will likely never be on that list, as they are not nurtured to swing. Nothing is kneading them to swing, concentrating or stimulating the vote and its distribution. Some swing more freely than others. Still, they swing, with Florida perhaps making the most pendulous swipes. The remaining thirty-eight states are considered as "safe" states in which a party's win is entirely predictable. However, safe is the old normal, and I predict that the list of swing states will continue to grow to the point where the term will lose its gravity, and with it, the base of its swing.

* * *

The concept of a super-delegate grew out of the aftermath of the riotous 1968 Democratic National Convention. Vice President Hubert Humphrey won the nomination of his party without entering a single primary. As a result, changes were made in the delegate selection process to rectify what was seen to be a sense of control over the nomination process by primary voters. In 1970, Representative Don Fraser (D-MN) and Senator George McGovern formed a commission. The idea was to create a delegation system that was less candidate-centered and more reflective of votes cast in primary elections. The McGovern-Fraser Commission resulted in an increase in the number of primary races held for a general election, from a mere seventeen in 1968 to thirty-five in 1980. It was the democratic thing to do, proactive in the way of giving candidates, as well as voters, that fair shake. It did, however, aide in the shellacking of McGovern by Nixon in 1972 and Jimmy Carter by Reagan in 1980. By 1981, in an effort to further refine the nomination process, the voting paradox fell in the hands of Governor James Hunt (D-NC). He assembled a commission that advanced the idea of a "super-delegate," unelected and unpledged delegate slots for Democratic members of Congress. The percentage of these delegates, these "swing" voters, was set to be thirty. By the first election (1984) to incorporate it into the nomination process, it had dwindled to fourteen. It increased over time to 20 percent by 2008.

Super Tuesday is a special day to politically astute Americans, some of whom might have even consented at their caucus to be a delegate. Typically, the most (34 percent) of the available pledged delegates are awarded to a candidate this day. In the 2020 election cycle, superdelegates made up roughly 16 percent of the Democratic Party delegates. By definition, not committed to vote for a candidate the system has been the seed of much controversy over the years. It was perceived that in 2016 Clinton was being favored in her race against Bernie Sanders as a number of superdelegates pledged their support for her early in the campaign. With Joe Biden the "presumptive" nominee, the point is all but moot. If Sanders, or any of the plethora of candidates, remained by the Democratic National Convention (which may only take place virtually), the superdelegates would not have voted on the first ballot unless there is no doubt about the outcome. As it turns out, thanks mostly to a pandemic, there isn't. I blame Sander's campaign suspension on three things. The pandemic and its limitations on effective campaigning, the reticence of voters to be progressive in the face of Trump, and the lack of resonance with black voters. For Biden, or the other presumptive candidate, to have won on the first ballot, he would have had to secure a majority of pledged delegates during the primary contests and caucuses preceding the Democratic National Convention. A candidate must win 1,991 of the available 3,379 delegate votes. Sanders dropped out of the race in early April, amidst concerns of COVID-19, which had been declared latently by Trump to be a national emergency (a man who once declared building a border wall to be a national emergency in order to justify funding). The centrist and the progressive, the mainstream and aged creek less taken, to avoid the assumptions of inequality of 2016, reached a compromise. Sanders could keep hundreds of votes that would normally have been forfeited by dropping out. As I had hoped from the beginning, the two men ultimately saw the bigger picture. Defeating Donald Trump was their focus, not advancing either of their agendas. According to party rules, because Biden was the sole contender, Sanders should have forfeited one-third of his accumulated votes. In the face of the rule, Biden is insistent that Sander retain his pledged delegates for the convention in August.

Bitterness developed between Sanders and Clinton in 2016, a factor in the protracted equation of what led to her losing the White House to the least qualified individual ever to win it. Biden's rapport with Sanders is vastly different, more amenable, and less contested. After three and a half years of watching Democracy assaulted on a daily basis, the US standing in the world reduced to that of a developing nation, a mockery made of every federal office, and the trust of our allies damaged or lost, the tone of primary debates (for the most part) was pragmatic in their pitch to defeat Trump. By May, Biden had accumulated 1,046 delegate votes, surging after a resurrecting win in the South Carolina primary. Sanders had gathered 974 votes, although polls stopped counting after he dropped out in early April. With numerous endorsements, including most of his opponents, Biden's decision of vice president remains as probably one of the most critical in history. That alone can compromise itself (or him) and create a bridge from centrist to progressive, from mainstream old-school Democrat to socialist. To the White House, Biden could bring a woman, a woman of color, or a woman with the progressiveness of Sanders, like Elizabeth Warren. He treads a thin line, risking the alienation of a bloc of disgraced Republicans who have a racial bone in their body. An article in May suggested that Republicans might be lost if his VP choice was Stacey Abrams. In their judging eyes, she has committed the cardinal sin of black women. Referring to her race with Kemp, she did not accept the legitimacy of an election won by means of voter suppression, and she refuses to be accordingly docile and humble. Representative—and Trump impeachment manager—Val Demmings, Senator Kamala Harris, and former Obama security advisor and UN ambassador Susan Rice are the other black women up for the job. Biden is left with making a critical decision in the wake of the most destructive presidency in modern history—and no, Nixon does not even come close. His decision will bind the exit wounds, tell a lot about what kind of president he will be, but most importantly, it will determine voter turnout. Biden's VP choice will be the exponent that can have the ability to move the American electorate to the left enough to not serve up Donald Trump another marginal electoral win.

VII. True Democracy: A Reason to Dream

The vote is the most powerful instrument devised
by man for breaking down injustice and destroying
the terrible walls which imprison men because they
are different from other men.

—Lyndon B Johnson

In southern border towns like Irvine, Texas, migrants wait in offices to become citizens, American citizens with a vote. A monitor at the front of the office contorts lurching images Donald Trump pitching the snake oil that "No matter where you come from or what faith you practice, this country is now your country." To further irritate the viscous patter, he adds, "Our history is now your history and our traditions are now your traditions. You enjoy the full rights and sacred duties that come with American citizenship. Very, very special." This is the soft sell, by a class-A huckster and IV-F draft dodger no less. The hopeful migrants raise their right hands to take the Oath of Allegiance. Sounds of dreams yearning to commence jettison the room in unison:

I hereby declare that I absolutely and entirely
renounce and abjure all allegiance and fidelity to
any foreign prince, potentate, state, or sovereignty.

They are in the club. They will soon be registered to vote, likely against the man they just watched condemn their history and traditions. They read the Constitution. They know their rights. But this is the defining moment, precisely why these huddled masses (or now socially distanced masses) have come to America despite its repellent, repugnant, and repressive history. To vote in a limited democracy and have a greatly homogenized chance of changing things. Like many things in the good old USA, the vote is processed, wrapped and packaged. Yet one must believe the predicate of righting the wrongs and the injustices of history. They came to this troubled abode wanting to follow the cues of patriots, movers, and shakers, from Samuel Adams to MLK, to Shirley Chisholm and Barack Obama. Step one of the fabled American dream is complete. The carrot is hung. Problem is that at no other time in recent history have the components of that dream been in such jeopardy of being compromised, limited, or taken away completely—particularly if you are not a natural citizen. And the irony is the migrants know their constitutional rights, many times better than the natural citizens.

The newly dubbed, "oathinized," formulized citizen can register to vote right there, at the induction office, a recruitment for democracy's army. The new American also has the option of registering online in thirty-eight states. In eleven states, a citizen becomes eligible when they reach legal age. Or, for the skittish American, unsure if they want to participate in the "experiment" of democracy, twenty-one states leave the option of registering the day of the election. Texas stands alone. The art of voter suppression, or the potential for it, is as perfected as their barbeque. The suspecting deputized voter can fill out a form and mail, or physically present it, to the county's voter registrar office. They could also register with an official volunteer at the office of immigration, providing that volunteer has been deputized in the same county in which the new citizen resides. For example, a deputized registrar can register people at a naturalization ceremony in Dallas County, providing they were deputized in Dallas Country. They cannot register relations who reside in Kaufman County. There are 254 counties in Texas, and the city of Dallas is a part of five of them. The voter's logistics are impaired. A move across town could require them to register to vote again, and for this, they must find the registrar deputized in the proper county. So, a solution to this voting conundrum is for the registrar to get deputized in as many counties as possible. As a VDR (voluntary deputy registrar), seeking such status in multiple counties presents ,problems. They are required to deliver acquired voter registration forms to the relevant county election office in person, during hours of business and, they are invalid after five days of completion. Nice. A glitch in the American dream in its infancy (a telltale of a democratic cradle spun, but that's another story). These are Texas laws, not debatable, by which VDRs are bound. To register a new voter, a soldier in the democratic army, a donkey following the carrot, a VDR could conceivably accrue a significant gas bill. After the acquired registrations have made it through the channels of perpetuity to the county election office, they are subject to frailties. The handwritten forms must be entered, individually, into voter rolls. In the case that the form is unclear (a person might have a flare to their lettering foreign to the eyes of an English speaking worker), or if it is not complete, ideally, the election office will contact the prospective voter to clarify the error. I wonder what the record of "ideal" is in Texas when the law is concerned. Welcome to America, land of opportunities to fall through bureaucratic cracks.

The voter registration system in Texas is fraught with inefficiencies, possibilities for suppression, discrimination, or abject nullification. Along with menacingly stringent voter ID laws, the economically inefficient registration procedure is a reason for the low voter turnout in the state. It would make sense that having people be able to vote would be in the interest of a politician (as was the case May 13, 2020, in Wisconsin), but evidently, Texas does not follow that logic. It is simple. According to a reliable contemporary history, when Democrats control things, an effort is made to facilitate voting for the most people and maximize turnout. Reciprocally, when Republicans are in control, an equal effort is made to make voting, even registering, difficult and minimize the turnout. It is this cross-purpose duality that compels a vital component of the American dream. Due to the arduous work of 3,100 VDRs in Dallas County, for the first time in its history, Texas has more than sixteen million registered voters in 2020.

It's perplexing, the daunting specter of voting. How fraught with fragilities for rejection or suppression something we as (white) natural-born Americans take for granted must be to an immigrant on their foray to the polls. Especially in the age of Trump, when stories of the ICE men coming for deportation permeate the news, it could well be a terrifying exercise. Voters of color, or other national origin, in the context of voting primarily, are really living in a fool's paradise in 2020. They are the rued huddled masses now swaddled and coddled in the auspices of a de facto constitution when amendments and their clauses amount to 231-year-old "in theories." The voter faces being denied their vote because; they lack the proper ID, their registration is expired, their signatures aren't a match, or they have done time in prison and have not paid their fines in full. If a voter is of African American, Latino, or Asian heritage, or even if their name has a sound of one of these ethnic groups, their names stand a good chance of being purged from voter rolls.

Many states allow people to vote early, as many as forty-six days prior to an election. Some states allow early voting with certain restrictions. At least twenty-two states allow early voting without restrictions. Missouri, Mississippi and Alabama allow no early voting. Some states now allow ex-felons to vote on the completion of their sentence. Some states it is a blanket allowance, while others either select upon eligibility or disallow felons to vote ever. Also, in recent years, due to voter fraud, irregularities ranging from suppression to collecting votes from the dead, states have debated how the voter needs to identify him or herself.

Voter ID requirements by state

No ID required	Requested but not required	Strict requirements
WA, OR, CA, NV, WY, NE, MN, IL, NC, MD, NJ, CT, MA, NY, NH, ME, NM, PA, VT	IA, SD, MT, ID	AZ, TX, KS, MO, IN, AS, KY, TN, AL, GA, OH, WI, FL, UT, CO, ND, OK, LA, SC, MS, MI, WV, VA, DE, AK, HI

All these precursors, the many caveats to being allowed to do what was inferred from the oath spoken in becoming an American citizen, help explain why, out of thirty-two developed nations, the US ranks twenty-sixth in voter turnout. It is no accident the USA is not number one in the league of voting. There is a definite design flaw in the blueprint for democracy for a government by the people. (Was that custom made by the people?) When Thomas Jefferson quilled the Declaration of Independence, he included a thought about voting: "Governments are instituted among Men, deriving their just Powers from the Consent of the Governed." Okay, a somewhat caustic implication of voting, of governments consisting of men who are empowered by those men they govern. Jefferson was the big proponent of states' rights, of states deciding for themselves ethical matters such as slavery or voting. For example, from 1797 to 1807, New Jersey's constitution allowed women to vote—if they owned land. The question remained, critical to Jefferson's intention; how would Americans consent to be governed, who should vote, and how should they vote? The possibilities were mulled, even debated, and thought was given to minority voting. In colonial times, worrying about minority rights simply raised the concern that the property owners would be over-run by non-property owners, the haves being bested or equaled by the have-nots. That is an impossible proposition to the human condition. More than two centuries later, the situation is fundamentally the same, and if Trump gets another term, I surmise it will be exactly the same. I digress.

The right of suffrage, as James Madison wrote, is a fundamental Article in Republican Constitutions. At the same time, the regulation of that right requires much attention. He saw that if the right to vote was extended only to property owners, there would always be a group to feel the sting of oppression. If the right was extended to all, the property owners risked being over-run by a majority without property. Voting as a right materialized as amendments in each case, decades after the fact. The Fourteenth, Fifteenth, Nineteenth, Twenty-sixth Amendments, and legislation to enforce them, were necessary to give all Americans a fair shake in voting.

Nothing that pertains to an individual's right to vote is in the crux of the US Constitution. The architects of this document, of the very plan for a democracy, which by definition implies a governance *by* the people, an achievement coming from exercise by those people "directly or indirectly through a system of representation usually involving periodically held free elections," left voting to the states. The key component of a democracy was, perhaps intentionally, left out of the original document signed by a representative from each of the thirteen colonies and made the law of America for the next 231 years. Instructions were included, however, on how it could be amended, almost as if that necessity were implicit. A consensus of three-fourths of the states could add to, or repeal from (21st), the Constitution. As I mentioned earlier, the broken record is used. Its relative state of complacency is like the transcendence of a skip from an old 45, or how the click of mid-song 8-track learns to fit in an ear.

Article I, section 4 of the Constitution leaves the times, place, and manner of elections to the state. The collective intellect of those benevolent Founders surely intuited that this was bound to lead to unfair voting practices. Like the Bible, the Constitution seems to have intentionally left many things vague, obfuscated, ameliorative, and prone to the free will of man. It is as though the Founders of the Constitution, the architects of American democracy, had a faith that man would do the right thing. At its writing, the only voters were wealthy white men. History paints a less than positive picture of Andrew Jackson, but it was "Old Hickory" himself who helped advance the political rights of the common man who did not own land. It was not until 1860 that white male non-landowners had voting rights. For the next 160 years, blacks, women, Native Americans, non-English speakers, and citizens between age eighteen and twenty-one fought for voting rights. They are fights, uphill, and for a few of those groups, the trajectory (kind of like the US COVID curve as long as Trump is in) is never downward. Was it an honest mistake, an oversight, a gross miscalculation of a potential government? Could those drafters, in their odorous powdered wigs, have seen the consequences of leaving voting up to states?

I am inclined to believe Article I, section 4, was written in a similarly contemporaneous context as the Second Amendment. Read in full, something I doubt has been done since the corruption of the NRA in the early 1970s; it is clearly implicit that the right to bear arms extends only to the people who comprise the militia, which in 1793 was the common man. The parameters around which voting evolved were written with a far less diverse population in mind; white males of means. The Electoral College was a product of its time, counting the slave as three-fifths of a man for its purposes. Sure, with a much smaller demographic, a much more concentrated majority at the spigot, it is much easier to regulate the water's flow, to ensure that each participant gets his fair share. It is entirely conceivable that, cognizant of the only contending parties in the voting, for the founders' foreseeable future, that Article I, section 4 could be a functional system leaving a negotiable margin of error.

It always comes screaming back to me, in illusory hieroglyphics, that our democracy errs on the side of human frailty. The Founders gravely underestimated the fallibility of voters, of people given free-will, of the penchant for irrational judgment, cruelty, oppression, even depravity. The proof is before us, every day, preaching nonsensical self-indulgent babble, weighing the potential of a Lysol IV drip to kill COVID-19. The irony is that, in a time when medical treatment was to bleed the ill with leaches, and medical options were limited, the "what have you got to lose" philosophy may have been embraced. But it happens, and Trump is the worst case, in a limited democracy. It happens in one that is indirect and "strains" the election process through an entity supposedly designed to prevent such things as a mentally deranged populist assuming absolute power. Voting is left to the states where it stands the most chance of being fairly represented, but also of being suppressed, rigged, swayed, or corrupted. When you cast your vote for president, you are actually voting for an elector (who will later, unless they are faithless, vote for that candidate) who was previously selected by a state legislature, the members of which you directly voted for once. So, in a sense, if one considers how that elector got there, they are voting directly in the general election. That would indeed be a watered-down watershed moment. America's electoral system leaves a significant margin for error, for any intention a voter, or the collective voters had, to fall through the cracks. But that is the system, for better or worse, the internal struggle on which democracy thrives—or is complacently, wontedly, perhaps willfully, deprived.

America was founded by giving advantages to some, while leaving other select groups vulnerable to be oppressed, suppressed, to end as targets for discrimination. It's diabolical in its passive-aggressive parlance, the Constitution. It gives instructions on how a predetermined percentage of states can amend it, yet the votes of each state can be suppressed by a dominant party. But even if an amendment, the fifteenth, for instance, is ratified and made federal law, it is still subject to interpretation by each state. The law is not even a law in the quarter of the states where the amendment did not pass, as was the case in Maryland in 1922. The state had rejected passing the amendment giving women suffrage, later (1941) passing it. Two years after it had met the required three-fourths of the states for passage, two women were sued attempting to vote in Baltimore. The case went to the US Supreme Court, where the amendment was upheld, on technicalities of the Constitution's earlier amendments. The system is a work in progression and digression, a subject of many varying factors and trends, lobbies, donors, and special interest groups. Founders left voting to the states, effectively providing a backdoor for the seemingly endless parade of unscrupulous politicians, waxing and waning in severity, who have waltzed through history stepping on the most vulnerable populations' rights. Lyndon Johnson signed a voting rights act in 1965, only after his mandate of the previous year left blacks still suppressed and intimidated at the polls after they were confronted by southern state troopers on the Edmund Pettus Bridge. The 1965 act aimed to remedy that suppressed vote by requiring states with a history of discrimination to submit any new voting laws to the justice department (an act that today would lack any real purpose). The provision was struck down by the Supreme Court in 2013. Times had changed, they ruled, and without skipping a moment of that time, the states reverted right back to the discriminatory practices that had worked so well for them, that had kept the carrot moving.

* * *

A take-away from the Dickens novel *Great Expectations* is that having a moral conscience is more important in the scheme of things than social advancement, wealth, or class. The expectations of the common American, the typical dream weaver, has diminished precipitously, certainly in recent years. Democrats stick to the moral high ground, slipping to echo Michelle Obama's 2016 advisory "when they go low, we go high." Republicans of late have rarely let us down, gravitating to the low road like the needle of a defective moral compass. The Trump-era has brought levels of depravity, hypocrisy, and corruption that make Nixon look like a rouge boy scout. I grew up in the shadow of Vietnam and Watergate and expect little from government. But when Republicans are at the spigot, my expectations are even lower. In April 2020, they attempted to keep voters from the poll by pitting their health and safety against the right to vote, the urge to prevent a Trump-endorsed incumbent Republican state judge from winning his seat of ten years in Wisconsin's Supreme Court. They went low again, and their tired bag of tricks did not work. After Democratic governor Tony Evers tried to postpone the election due to the pandemic, Republicans blocked him through the state supreme court. Delay of the contest was disallowed, successfully blocking mail-in votes, and allowing in-person voting. Masked voters went to the polls, risking the spread of COVID-19 (and cases, as well as deaths, were soon traced to this event), and waiting in socially distanced lines, in some cases in the rain. These are the truest Americans, preserving democracy, exercising their right to vote, even when it is facing suppression with the direst consequences. Their fortitude and patriotism defeated Justice Daniel Kelly and put liberal Dane County judge Jill Karofsky on the Supreme Court. I expect they will go low in November.

Washington, Oregon, Utah, Colorado and Hawaii have for years been voting by mail. Republicans have stood by it, practiced it, even encouraged it. Donald Trump, as well as many of his staff, votes by mail. The argument that it is an opening to fraud is supported by virtually zero evidence. I personally prefer to vote in person if possible, having voted by absentee ballot once, and never in a general election. If we are in the same COVID-19 circumstances in November (and I choose to be), and Trump grasps at his last straws of suppression in his pathetic narcissistic desperation to win, I plan to mask up, cinch my hood tight around my face, put on dark glasses, and go to the polls looking like the uni-bomber. Yes, an ironic situation is there. Mail-in voting has been around and widely embraced by both parties a lot longer, I'm sure, than Donald J. Trump. It was Lincoln, the name behind the party the South once moved toward, the party he turned into a den of inequities, who offered mail-in voting for men fighting the Civil War. Like most avenues gone down routinely in the interest of facilitating democracy, Donald Trump weaponized mail-in voting. Lincoln allowed soldiers to vote from the battlefield, and it was the Democrats (the future Republicans) who protested, claiming widespread fraud and a Republican "scheme" devised to "gain some great advantage to their party." This was said as by a Wisconsin state senator just as the legislature, in a party-line vote, made the state the first to legalize absentee voting. In the 1864 presidential election, roughly 150,000 of the 1,000,000 Union soldiers voted via absentee ballot. It was a novel virtual vote, the first in history, and changed the course and participation of democracy.

A century and a half later, a different type of war, a global conflagration waged by a natural combatant immune to surrender, once again necessitates massive mail-in voting. An accidental president, illegitimate, hostile, desperate to have his constitutional second term, seized the day. He is probably the only living American president who could or would make a pandemic more deadly than it is. So, voting by mail is hardly a twentieth-century idea, having been a much-practiced option for military and in many states. However, in 2020, when COVID-19 droplets permeate the air, when people wear masks and afford six feet of leeway, a soldier holed in a cave in Afghanistan can vote more easily than a black soldier on R & R in San Diego. Virtual voting is as old as this country. There is a record of members of the Continental Army while fighting the British in 1775 who were able to vote by proxy at a town hall in Hollis, New Hampshire. Reflected in the history of absentee voting in America lie all the major wars in which it has involved itself. Politicians, whether it's for noble or self-indulgent reasons, have made sure that the people fighting their wars did not feel disenfranchised. In the worst years of the Civil War, election officials in Pennsylvania were sent to encampments to construct rudimentary polling facilities. The states that allowed such enfranchising efforts were Republican controlled. Democrats objected to this broadening of the voting potential. That objection alone found encouragement far rampant voting by mail, via absentee ballot or simply allowing a soldier to send a letter to a proxy back home. People marked their ballot, stuffed it in an envelope, and sent it to the county that had registered them to vote. A county official would then drop the ballot in a box with all the other votes where they were counted on election eve. By WWII, as Democrat was in the embryonic stages of its decades-long transformation to Republican, as interests and motives of each party began to change, all states allowed mail-in voting. Military, in 1944, was responsible for 3.2 million of the votes cast, roughly seven percent of the electorate, which won FDR a fourth term.

For the last 150 years, opponents to any kind of virtual voting have cited its potential for "gross fraud," not unlike Donald Trump's purely politically motivated machinations today. *Nation*, a publication in 1866, cautioned that "No law has been devised in any state in which suffrage has been given to citizens in military service that did not leave room for the grossest of frauds." It appealed to the basest human interaction, "Every safeguard by which legislation has striven to preserve the purity of franchise is thrown down; and, as human nature, the inevitable tendency is to inaugurate a system of fraud." It aimed low, reflecting Democratic (next century's Republican) motives, their effort to control and manipulate voting, which has endured as the go-to election strategy of the ideology. There exists, however, virtually no instances, as far back as the Civil War, to support the claim of fraud. In the midst of a pandemic, with the threat of a virus highly communicable through airborne pathogens, Trump is blocking the routine practice of mail-in voting, of absentee voting, of proxies, any method that is alternative to live voting. He is hoping that America will favor their health over casting votes that will most assuredly spell defeat for him.

I cannot fathom how anyone with half a mind, a will to live, and any regard for the lives of anyone else can vote for him. Democracy is on the critical list. The Constitution is in shreds, with lines blurred, perverted, customized as much as those "Christian" Republicans (god love 'em) tender obscure passages in the Bible to justify almost anything. Donald Trump is truly a Gumpish figure, right down to his spurred feet. Like Forrest, Trump was a ne'er-do-well with a finite IQ who bumbled through his own delusion of what America's history has been, what its presence is, and what its future can and should be. Yet, as sure as virus droplets circulate in the stale air of planes, there will be a small contingency of Americans who will vote for Trump. They will vote for him and may (or may not) worsen their own situation. Those are the unintelligible ones, or just plainly idiotic, too dense to realize a vote for their bronze pope is not going to benefit them in any way. Their votes will also unquestionably imperil the situation for fellow Americans and fellow humans worldwide. Of course, they are either too dumb or too self-absorbed to know this. They will exponentially increase the chance of their or someone they know, or even love, the chance of contracting COVID-19 and dying. It is a calculable equation; the odds of getting a highly contagious virus in four years in the charge of a government who fails its expected role in every capacity versus a government in the charge of a man who has proven experience suppressing pandemics. In May, Columbia University estimated Trump's sloth, denial, maliciousness, inexperience, and ignorance caused 36,000 deaths. Start with that as a base. Add to that the deaths caused by unchecked nursing facilities, prisons, the forced working of packing plants, and the religious zealots kneeling together in church Petri dishes praying for the viral spread to end. Figure the cluster rate, how a handful of Americans, how a few governors and mayors take the word of Trump rather than Anthony Fauci or any scientist, doctor, or epidemiologist. Figure the Ozark pool parties, the MAGot protests to open and do business, to "give me liberty or give me COVID-19." Figure in the indoor no-mask-required rallies as Trump puts on another layer of BRONZO and hits the campaign trail. Consider the fall-out, the bottom-of-the-barrel rapacious MAGots yelling "Lock her up" as drops of Lysol soaked COVID droplets slip through their spaced teeth. Subtract any one of these contributory factors, and the odds of contracting COVID-19 in a forty-eight-month sentence go down precipitously. These are all reasons, rationales, justifications, for the wounded elephant's thrashing, his aberrant tweets, his tolerance of violence, and contemptuous response to anything that lies in his path to reelection.

* * *

More than a century ago, a president commandeered a nation. It was engaged in a world war, and a group of women liked to call him "Kaiser Wilson." He was once burned in effigy. His success in the middle of his second term depended on the willingness of people to vote despite a pandemic, a "grippe" that was killing people, VAP, by the dozen in a day. The worst months of the Spanish flu were in the fall, September and October, in the weeks before the midterm election, November 5, 1918. In contention were the composition of the 66th Congress, women's suffrage, and on the ballot in at least eight states was alcohol prohibition. There were temperance activists, such as Ohio's Muskingum County Dry Federation, who accused the liquor industry of using the flu to profit off the "suffering and deaths of human beings." They argued that it was widely circulated that whiskey was a cure for the Spanish influenza, citing stories of the use of liquor in "alcohol baths" for flu patients and as a stimulant for ailing military men.

Then there were the suffragists, who in many ways were fortuitously helped in their cause by a combination of the war and the flu. The election of 1918 was an opportunity for women to advance their cause beyond the twelve states in which they had won the right to vote. By foot or by auto, women were out canvassing in cities despite deadly warnings of the flu. Women gathered in Nevada, a state where they had been allowed for four years to vote, and decried "Rebuke the Democratic Party!" lambasting the conservative Democratic-majority in the US Senate for not passing the National Suffrage Amendment earlier that year. They were called upon to work, first in efforts for the war in the absence of men, but also as the men returned sick or dying from the flu. Their role is even said to have put them in a position where Wilson began to see the necessity of their being able to vote.

Patriotism was invoked as a medium, a cudgel through which voting would take place. Some states suggested that doing this civic duty in the perils of a pandemic would most certainly support the war effort. As it happened, the armistice Germany signed came a mere six days after Election Day, the anticipation and foresight of that fact perhaps blurred by the rampant mortality rate of the flu. California, for example, was peaking in its death rates and still ran this line in the *Los Angeles Times*,

EVERY LOYAL CALIFORNIAN WILL CAST VOTE at ELECTION

NO ELECTION QUARANTINE

Because of rumors, the state board of health has found it necessary to issue an official denial that it intends to stop tomorrow's elections under the rule against congregating. The elections will be held as usual.

The noble intentions lost in the end. Prudence bested politics. North Dakota health authorities suggested the "unheard of possibility of postponing the general election," as they faced over 15,000 influenza cases. A *Tampa Times* headline read, "Flu Vs. Ballot," warning that the virus was non-partisan. Interestingly, in Ohio, the media projected adamantly that the election would go on, with the *Marion Star* proclaiming, "Flu Ban or No Flu Ban."

A much-diminished 40 percent VAP masked up and braved the

polls. As today, social distancing was the order. No mention of mail-in or absentee ballots. So, to exercise their vote, people during the 1918 pandemic were also forced to forfeit their health. Granted, it was a midterm election and the stakes, the consequences of not voting, were not proportionate. Turnout was low, with many voters too ill to get to the polls or having to stay home to care for others. An analysis estimated that the drop in voter turnout between 1914 and 1918, due to the flu, was at least 10 percent. Republicans gained 25 seats in the House, ending the coalition control. They also netted a small margin, giving them control in the Senate.

WEAR MASK WHEN VOTING

City health officer JP Evaus of Pacific Grove urges everyone who goes to the polls tomorrow to wear a mask. All the election officials will be protected with masks, and others are requested to take the same precaution against Spanish Influenza.

EVERYBODY SHOULD VOTE TOMORROW

No one should remain away from the polls tomorrow on account of Spanish Influenza. Go to the polls and cast a vote for William D. Stephans for governor, C.C. Young for Lieutenant governor, and E.A Hayes for Congress

Any lesson to be learned from history was lost on the Trump Administration. Any semblance of governance not based in self-indulgence is foreign to the man and the insane immoral minions who follow him like tiny ass-kissing pilot fish. With all the technology available in the twenty-first century, a safe election in a pandemic would be possible to defeat any other president. It is truly the swamp bottom dweller, the pathetic border-line human, who uses a highly contingent virus to his political advantage. He misses, or ignorantly, lazily, dismisses the points, the acts, the lessons of history that might be good for America, a republic, or even democracy. He refused to use the Defense Protection Act to supply hospitals and first responders with protective equipment and ventilators to mitigate a virus his inaction and rhetoric caused and continues to cause to spread. Yet on June 1, 2020, to ameliorate the peaceful protests sparked by the George Floyd death, he found a 213-year-old Insurrection Act. It is a clause, rarely used, allowing federal troops to attack the people. He did invoke the Posse Comitatus Act of 1878 to bring the active troop into the District of Columbia to tear gas and pepper the peaceful protesters surging towards the White House, through Lafayette Park, at which point Trump grabbed his Bible and headed to boarded-up St. John's church for a photo op. You cannot write this stuff. Yet here I am, in 2020, writing this account of the exploits of the real-life Forrest Gump in the oval office. Vote, Americans, vote!

Epilogue

As I pray for a crushing Trump defeat in November, a 1964 level shellacking of a "Republican," I reserve the reality gleaned from 2016. I reserve a modicum of pessimism, that sliver of soap that tells me, pesters me incessantly, that I best prepare for the small chance of another electoral win. As poppy Bush used to say, not doing so "wouldn't be prudent." If Biden wins, even by 50 percent, Trump will balk. He will throw a tantrum, tweet a storm, hold his breath, and order Bill Barr to investigate the election commission for fraud. America will be lucky if it knows its president by Christmas. Even if Biden clearly and soundly defeats Trump, we will be as much in doubt as to who will occupy the White House as we were in 2000. Either way, it will not be pretty. If Trump wins, America's days are over. If he loses, the most litigious, acrimonious, and hateful transition in presidential history is at hand. He will not go gently into that good night is an understatement. It is, at best, a poetic paraphrase that begs for more.

This time in history is bifurcated. There is a palpable feeling of fear, but there is an equally tangible feeling of hope. The protests following the surrealistically atrocious and anomalous death of George Floyd under the knee of a senior Minneapolis police officer yielded concrete signs of a change in systemic racism in America. It also yielded the most feared, but most unhinged (a likely Achille's heal) moment from Donald Trump. Never in my fifty-five years have I seen a man desecrate the Constitution and pimp out the Bible for his own gain in a "fire at peaceful protesters" quenchable moment. The invocation of the Posse Comitatus Act of 1878 that June night will live in infamy. It was met with bewilderment and initially dismissed as some crazed impulse by defense secretary Mark Espers. He, and other Senate Republicans, neither condoning nor discouraging his deranged power grab, his constitutional blackmail effort to get votes. As it was denounced as slavishly contradictory to the essence of the Constitution by General Mattis, his threat to invoke the obscure 1807 Insurrection Act was most likely the tempered tantrum of a petulant and bitter president. If in Trump's waning days it did, if the mounting parallels to Hitler many wrote of as the twisted mindset of a chronic narcissist are rationalized, our idea of democracy that was supplanted two centuries ago will indeed be uprooted. If such a dystopia ever materialized, if a failed narcissist who ran as a populist ever succeeded in preventing the Constitution to sanction a war on the American people, the fundamental "baked-in" ideals of democracy will be lain bare, lost, left for the hawks and vultures to pick at, to scavenge the spaces where doves and eagles once flew. It is a sobering hypothetical, a greatly disturbing scenario that even American art has never imitated. Coupled with 100,000 deaths that continue from COVID, unemployment that can easily surpass levels of the Great Depression, and no real end in sight for either, America is ripe for the breaking, weakened by natural and man-made crises. But often, if that weakness touches the right people, ordinary people who have the spirit that moved Samuel Adams, Alice Paul, or Cesar Chavez, strength can be found. The trappings, the logistical limitations that are in effect to stem the spread of COVID-19, created a vacuum. Ironically, it induced a yearning to breathe, to perhaps taste a better life for Americans whose ancestors, we blanketly forget, never willfully came here in the first place.

For 401 years, since the first Africans arrived as slaves in the Jamestown colony in 1619, there has been a learning curve aimed facetiously at incrementally narrowing section of white America. It has been, during that time, more like a tidal wave, which advances and recedes with the sustained culpability to teach for which one uses a metronome. Thus, evolved two Americas, white and black, with corresponding systems of justice, voting, transportation, interstate commerce, any function of American society that could be amended in fact, up to and including using the bathroom (Jim Crow). The conspiratorial factoid of white privilege is only augmented by someone like Trump, whose very existence at all is a result of the most privilege in the oval since Kennedy. It has been dispersed like a numbing mace over a decade, resulting in often fatal incidents of brutality of black citizens in the twenty-first century that rivals the incidents of lynching in the nineteenth and twentieth centuries.

Art is imitative of life. Movies, literature, music reflect what is wrong, what is immoral, what cries out for justice in America. In 1960 Harper Lee published *To Kill a Mockingbird*, a fictional work that depicts the racial injustices faced by blacks in the 1950s Deep South. The fundamental attitudes and blind spots that created those inequities, those abysmal gaps between white and black justice that were facts on which that fiction was based, sixty years ago, are present and (not) accounted for today. A "true crime" novel, *The Lynching's in Duluth*, came out in 2000. It accounted, finally, the 1920 lynching of a black man accused of raping a white woman. Duluth, Minnesota, is roughly 150 miles north of Minneapolis and St. Paul, cities that bear the shame of being the sites of systemic brutality based on race in cases such as the 2016 St. Paul shooting of Philando Castile, the Georgia shooting of Ahmaud Arbery in February 2020, and the asphyxiation of George Floyd in May 2020 in Minneapolis. I grew up in the shadow of a city that was, and is, a bastion of racism, an ignorance of the black man I expected might be noticeably less in a state this far north. It's here; it's everywhere. The South just wears it on their sleeves, sheets and hoods. The racial history of the Twin Cities reads like *Black like Me*, Duluth's past like *To Kill a Mockingbird*.

* * *

On February 3, 2020, lead Senate trial manager Adam Schiff stood in the well of the Senate to make his closing remarks. He tried one last time to salvage from Republicans that long lost purpose of America, what thousands had collectively fought and died for, for that party of Lincoln that had once lured southern Democrats. Donald Trump had been impeached in the House of Representatives. On December 18, 2019, a partisan vote had charged him with two Articles of Impeachment: obstruction of Congress and abuse of power. It seemed like a cogent culmination of a long, long, long list of acts of criminality, dishonesty, and exploitation of his position. It was a boiling down, perhaps thought to be a simplification that left Republicans little latitude for defense. There was none so, in a cowardly, due process defying move characteristic of many Republicans today, Majority Leader McConnell refused to hear witnesses. The party of Lincoln was mute, on its deathbed, lying in vain, not even willing to charge the president with the latest abuse of his power; his soliciting of Ukraine's help in maligning his opponent in November by withholding a favor. It is ironic that with that parcel of dirt, the allegations of the dealings of Hunter Biden with a corrupt company in Ukraine, in his quiver, the Trump campaign has failed to aim it at "sleepy" Joe. All that trouble, all the months of firings, resignations, and character assassinations, the risk of impeachment, have apparently been for nothing. It did provide an opportunity, a lapse in immorality. The wounded partisan, the white elephant sale in the room, had control this round. Utah senator Mitt Romney defected boldly and voted with Democrats to convict. As Donald Trump lapped up his acquittal, Schiff closed that great miscarriage of justice. He was sure the president would do it again would repeat his successful tit for tat, quid pro quo game plan. It came, less than two months after his glorious acquittal. On March 28, 2020, Trump held COVID-19 aide from Michigan's governor Gretchen Witmer because she was not sufficiently appreciative. In his closing of the Senate trial, Schiff also alluded to how bad things in America could get, hinting at the incrementally worse strangulations of democracy this incorrigibly irresponsible, inexperienced, accidental president was capable of if allowed to continue as commander in chief. The June biblical photo op, the grabbing power by the Posse Comitatus Act, the threatening to use an obscure and archaic act of insurrection to turn the US military on its citizens, that was how bad it could get. Those sad, pathetic, desperate, humorous, and frighteningly apocalyptic moves will be hard to top.

In June, Biden was leading Trump by 14 percent in a national poll, Biden being up five points and Trump being down four from an earlier poll. Romney, former President Bush, and Collin Powell won't be voting for Trump. Cindy McCain (widow of John, who I know would find Trump's latest actions egregious to any republic) will not vote Republican. Former House Speakers Paul Ryan and John Boehner, as well as another oscillating GOP not-wannabe's covertly curse Trump, wishing there were another GOP candidate. (They can still write-in Bill Weld.) They are the loyal crew of the Titanic, ignoring the band, in its final hour, in its chairs' umpteenth configuration, trying to avoid the watered-down death by politics. They are confined in their wait with a man, who has an ego as big as the iceberg and a conscience smaller than the first trickle of water to seep through the walls of the ship, to blink, surrender his position (he has to COVID), or lose in a legal battle in November. Former generals, many who had been cautiously complicit with Trump as members of his cabinet, denounced him in June. Calling the military, in his position as commander in chief, to use force on people every member took an oath to protect, to defend from foreign enemies, was too much for them to extend their former complicity. The oath of the president, the echoing words that fill, with varying degrees of sustainability, the air of DC every fourth January 20th is only slightly dissimilar to that spoken by every recruit to the US military. People in the business of war, of defending America, its citizens, and democracy from enemies foreign and domestic, found conflict, dissonance, in the suggestion by an equally sworn commander that troops be used to regulate Americans. Their support disappeared. By the second week of June, always the compellingly devious and malevolent chess player, Trump withdrew his latest black pawn, off which he had never totally removed his hands. Washington. DC, Mayor Muriel Bowser had the local franchise. As the killing of George Floyd had set off a wave of mostly peaceful protests against systemic racism in police departments, of brutality that has flown under the radar of "qualified immunity" for decades, she had the streets near the White House emblazoned with BLACK LIVES MATTER and DEFUND THE POLICE in thirty-five-foot tall yellow letters. This looked to me to be signs of a man who had lost what tenuous grasp he had on a pussy, if not the people, certainly those pro-life women who voted for him four years ago. It told me Trump's hope of a second term was over, and that the American electorate could now be influenced enough (by the opposition of top Republicans and military leaders, who MAGot sheep also follow for red meat snacks) to close the opportunity for his only chance of a narrow electoral victory.

George Floyd is a martyr [of Jesus level]. His death came at a point in time when several factors were loose in America and the world. Most importantly and immediately, there is the tipping point, the last straw, to allow police brutality born of systemic racism to continue as just a heated talking point. Then there is the one that is most appreciative, the environment. Floyd's death happened in the middle of a pandemic, in the throes of a nation yearning to be free, to reopen, to have a normal life again. So, there is that, the doubly suppressed rage, anger, and impetus to build a more perfect world, a more perfect union. There was the dichotomy of reopen versus stay sheltered-in-place, "liberate Minnesota" and "liberate Michigan" (with masked men brandishing weapons of war) versus masked homebound disciples of Dr. Fauci existing in six-foot increments. And then there's Trump himself, smugly vacant of any remorse for three and a half years of destroying policies of worth simply because many were made by a black man whose citizenship he challenged long before becoming president. Floyd gasped under the knee of an executive branch bottom-feeder, one who had undoubtedly scavenged off the toxic rhetoric of Trump (evidently long before) for his term, compounding decades of societal cues his profession tends to ignore that black lives matter. Mr. Floyd took a knee under a perfect storm. The recriminations of his abundantly unjustifiable death, "I can't breathe," the last gasps of a man calling out for his dead mother, a survivor of COVID-19 himself will, god willing, speak to the select remnants of white privilege infinitely in suggestion, in rueful incriminations, to the four officers hauntingly to their grave. And, if there is poetic justice, a rather large linebacker will take a knee on Chauvin's neck.

In the end, in America, with a salience for efficiency in its paths for errors in judgment and calculation, for human fallibility in calls of matriculation, is the vote. Its vulnerabilities to be discounted, suppressed, or simply denied are among the better reasons not to cast your vote, your GOP test line, into the sea of delusion. The stakes play out on the news each night, from abject failures to provide any trace of what a rational American human being has come to expect from a president, to levels of corruption and conflations of the Constitution that make Watergate look like a tea party. This November 3rd will be the 59th quadrennial General Election. The 58 that came before lacked the sense of urgency, the insidious sense of finality that I fear, an anxiety I am aware 80 percent of Americans share. No one living has experienced an election in which so much more than bigger government or smaller government, tax hikes for the rich or cuts to the middle-class is on the ballot. How about no government? How about slapping taxes on the backs of the working class, no questions asked, no representation? How about the end of democracy and the mantle of something more akin to North Korea? How about living in a country where a citizen like Otto Warmbier can be sentenced to fifteen years hard labor for taking a propaganda poster, in an America that even has propaganda posters for the taking? An America with zero opportunity (unless you are a wealthy white man) where human rights do not exist, where unidentified (Barr's recent Gestapo imitation) men brutally enforce laws, ICE men who round up brown-skinned people, where spaces exist someplace from which no one can hear you scream. You get the picture. It'd be ugly, repressive, grossly disenfranchising, and quite frankly I truly don't believe that even the most zealous of MAGots want to live like that, to be Sherman's as Mr. Peabody (Trump) sets his time machine for 1870, standing with waggling toothpicks still finding red meat morsels, for the next four years. Most MAGots are white, to be sure, but I don't think any are breaking the bank in blue collared shirts. Many rely on Medicare, maybe even the ACA, a few might even take social security in old age, and as these programs slip away, living the MAGA mentality would get old fast. The supply lines are drying up now. The further I got into this book, the more I felt like

I was writing a last will and testament for America as most readers know it. It is an obituary in the event one needs to be posthumously written. Simply put, a vote for Biden is a vote for democracy, and a vote for Trump is a vote for autocracy, a slope to a dictatorship. It boils down to a simple duality, a well-entrenched tribal dichotomy, because that is the most accessible human denominator. It is a story whose end—this one's—juxtaposes life over death; life of democracy (and the momentously envigored wave of the carrot) and humanity, or the death of it as well as 231 years of progression toward a "more perfect union." Toward that shining city on a hill, not the dumpster fire Trump referred to in his inaugural address. Vote [tight] America.

Bibliography

Barbash, Fred et. al, *The Washington Post*, "Federal Courts have ruled against Trump Administration Policies at least 70 Times," April 2019

Berg-Anderson, Richard E. 2010 Census State Populations and Distribution of Electoral Votes and Representatives

Bleifuss, Joel, *In These Times*, "In the 1968 DNC Protests, Did the Left Self-sabotage?" August 2018

Bomboy, Scott; *Constitution Daily*, "The one election where Faithless Electors made a difference," 2016

Chokshi, Niraj; *The New York Times*, "How the American Electorate is Changing," November 2016

Cillizza, Chris; "Sorry Hillary Clinton, the Electoral College isn't Going Anywhere," CNN Politics, September 2017

Cobb, Jelani; *The New Yorker*, "Voter-suppression Tactics in the Age of Trump," October 2018

Dembling, Sophia; *Sierra Magazine*, "Are you Registered to Vote? I sign up voters in Texas, a state that makes it as hard as possible" May 2020

Ember, Sydney; *The New York Times,* "Young Voters Could Make a Difference. Will they?," 2018

Engstrom, Erik J.; *Partisan Gerrymandering and the Construction of American Democracy*, University of Michigan Press, Ann Arbor, 2013

Erickson, Bo; CBS News, "Voting during a pandemic? Here's what happened in 1918," April 2020

Goldfield, David; The Gifted Generation: When Government was Good, HighBridge Books, 2017

Haag Matthew; *The New York Times*, "Mississippi Senator's 'Public Hanging' Remark Draws Backlash Before Runoff," November 2018

Katz, Marilyn; *In These Times*, "Blame the Democrats, Not the Protesters," August 2018

Kilgore, Ed; *New York Intelligencer*, "2018 Turnout Was the Highest of Any Midterm in More Than a Century," 2018

Lee, Kurtis; *Los Angeles Times* "In 1969, Democrats and Republicans united to get rid of the Electoral College. Here's what happened," December 2016

Little, Becky; History stories, "How the 'Party of Lincoln' Won Over the once Democratic South," August 2017

Parkinson, Hilary; *National Archives,* Pieces of History, "The Electoral College: Then and Now," 2012

Renda, Matthew; *Missoula Current*, "Biden and Sanders Reach Delegate Deal in Bid for Party Unity," May 2020

Rudin, Ken; *NPR political junkie*, "Who Gets The Blame For The Romney Loss? The Tea Party Has A Theory," November 2012

Sarlin, Benjy, NBC News, "Elizabeth Warren's plan to tax the super-rich has been tried before. Here's what happened." 2019

Seitz-Wald, Alex; NBC News, "How do you know voting by mail works? The U.S. military's done it since the Civil War," April 2020

Smith, Heather, *Sierra Magazine*, "Are States Trying to Stop Students from Voting? It's gotten much harder to vote on many campuses. Here's how to do it anyway," 2018

Stebenne, David; *Origins*, Current Events in Historical Perspective, "Re-mapping American Politics:

The Redisricting Revolution Fifty Years Later," February 2012

Tur, Katy: *Unbelievable*, Harper-Colins, New York, NY, 2017

Wade, Peter; *Rolling Stone*, "Trump Advisor Caught on Tape Dicussing 'Aggressive' Voter Suppression in 2020," December 2019

Weld, William and Levinson, Sanford; *USA Today*, "Winner-take-all presidential elections: "Unconstitutional and unfair to voters in 48 states," September 2019

Widmer, Ted; *The New Yorker*, "How the Census Changed America," May 2019

Wolfe, Michael: Fire and Fury: Inside the Trump White House, Henry Holt and Co., New York, 2018

About the Author

Amram's writing with Calumet began in 2017 and has been political in nature. Prior to publishing with them, he published several book in genres that range from poetry to short stories to historical fiction. In 2015 he was asked to read his poetry at the Loft's dedication as an International Peace Site. Amram's first book with Calumet, *Ten Years and Change: A Liberal Boyhood in Minnesota*, was entered as a nominee for the Minnesota Book Award.

Made in the USA
Middletown, DE
10 February 2022

60902706R00104